AISNE 1914

Battleground series:

Battleground Europe

AISNE 1914

Jerry Murland

First World War Series Editor
Nigel Cave

Pen & Sword
MILITARY

First published in Great Britain in 2013 by
Pen & Sword Military
an imprint of
Pen & Sword Books Ltd
47 Church Street
Barnsley
South Yorkshire
S70 2AS

Copyright © Jerry Murland 2013

ISBN 9781781591895

A CIP catalogue record for this book is available from the British
Library
Typeset in 10pt Times

Printed and bound in England by
CPI Group (UK) Ltd, Croydon, CR0 4YY
Pen & Sword Books Ltd incorporates the Imprints of Pen & Sword
Aviation, Pen & Sword Maritime, Pen & Sword Military, Wharncliffe
Local History, Pen and Sword Select, Pen and Sword Military
Classics, Leo Cooper, Remember When, Seaforth Publishing and
Frontline Publishing.

For a complete list of Pen & Sword titles please contact
PEN & SWORD BOOKS LIMITED
47 Church Street, Barnsley, South Yorkshire, S70 2AS, England
E-mail: enquiries@pen-and-sword.co.uk
Website: www.pen-and-sword.co.uk

CONTENTS

Introduction by the Series Editor

The BEF involvement in the Aisne area, from mid September to mid October 1914, has become something of a footnote in memory. It has been overshadowed by the drama of Mons and Le Cateau in August and the halting of the Germans at the Marne at the beginning of September; and then by the desperate fighting from La Bassée to Steenstraat, culminating in the exhausting, nerve wracking battles around Ypres and on the Messines Ridge in the dying days of October and the first two weeks or so of November. The Aisne has become, so to speak, a transit point between the battles and skirmishes of the Retreat and the Flanders battle.

Why this should be so is difficult to say. Perhaps it is because it was an area that was not to see British troops again until the perilous days of the early summer of 1918 – and even then it was only for a limited period. For the battlefield visitor, perhaps, it is a matter of distance and because it is seemingly so far away from the battlefields of the Somme, Arras and Flanders, each rich with the memory of the BEF for most of the war. Certainly one factor has been the relative paucity of guides to the BEF's Aisne battlefield, an area not notable for the number of those familiar signposts of the war, the cemeteries of the Commonwealth War Graves Commission.

Jerry Murland's book, I hope, will help to restore more interest in the BEF's contribution to this notable action; and of the units and men who fought, died and suffered here. The battle, officially from 12 – 15 September, followed by Actions on the Aisne Heights, 20 September and the Action of Chivy, 26 September, were bitterly fought engagements, taking place in difficult conditions; and casualties were very heavy. The Battle was the final attempt by the allies to follow through from the success of the Marne; and marks the successful establishment by the Germans of a sound defensive line on this part of the front: a front that was gradually, seemingly inexorably, becoming two lines of entrenched defensive positions. Hope for both sides now lay in enveloping actions to the north, each trying to get round the other's open flank, which resulted in a series of mutually bloody encounter battles until there was no flank left to envelop. Thus was the future character of warfare on the Western Front established; and it has its origins in this little known battlefield, in dramatic countryside, on the hills and fields either side of the River Aisne.

Nigel Cave
Stresa, October 2012

ACKNOWLEDGEMENTS

This book would not have been written if it had not been for the journal my grandfather kept of the war years. Amongst its pages he recorded the death of his great friend Captain Frank Hawes of 1/Leicesters, who was killed near Rouge Maison Farm on 23 September and of the letters he received from his cousin, Lieutenant Gerald Smyth, who was serving with 17/Field Company on the Aisne. It was these accounts that first led me to the area to see for myself where these two men had fought.

The writing of a book of this nature requires the help and support of a great many individuals and first and foremost I owe a great debt of gratitude to the men of the BEF who recorded their thoughts and experiences at the time, leaving a wonderful legacy for future generations of historians to read. Many of these accounts are held by the Imperial War Museum and to the staff in the reading room I extend my thanks for their kindness and patience. Members of staff at the National Archives at Kew have also provided much valued help and assistance as have those at the Leeds University Archive. I also thank the National Trust for their kind permission to publish the photograph of James Pennyman and Liz Godsell, who very kindly located and gave permission for the photograph of Kenneth Godsell to be published. Pen and Sword gave permission for extracts from *Fifteen Rounds a Minute* and the *Great War Diaries of Brigadier General Alexander Johnston* and the History Press gave permission to quote from *Tickled to Death to Go*. In all instances every effort has been made to trace the copyright holders where any substantial extract is quoted and the author craves the indulgence of literary executors or copyright holders where these efforts have so far failed.

The preparation of a book of this nature would have been impossible to write without following in the footsteps of the men of the BEF. To the stalwart individuals who have accompanied me on my numerous visits to the area I extend my thanks. Dave Rowland, Tom Waterer, Paul Webster and Bill Dobbs in particular have my thanks for their patience and company on what proved to be some highly entertaining and enjoyable battlefield visits. To Maurice Johnson goes my gratitude in giving me access to his personal Aisne archive and huge collection of photographs and postcards. Dave O'Mara produced a great collection of Aisne trench maps for me from his collection and Rebecca Jones had produced yet another set of maps for me. I must also thank Sebastian Lauder, who has helped enormously with the compilation of the

German ORBAT from official German accounts of the battle. Finally, and most importantly, I should like to thank my wife Joan for her patience and encouragement while I buried myself away writing and vanishing across the water to – as my nine years old granddaughter, Alisha, so eloquently puts it – to hang around cemeteries and find people who died a hundred years ago.

Jerry Murland. Coventry 2012

INTRODUCTION

THE FIRST BATTLE OF THE AISNE as defined by the Battles Nomenclature Committee began on 13 September 1914 and concluded two days later on 15 September. By nightfall on 15 September the front lines of the opposing forces had become more or less established; although the fighting had not stopped at that point, neither side made any further gains. However, as the stalemate situation gradually became established, the two sides did begin to dig in and resort to a war of intense shelling and local attacks – a situation that would become only too familiar over the next three years. Trench warfare had arrived.

Although British involvement in 1914 was a brief one compared to their French allies who fought in the valley for nearly four years, it remains a significant chapter in the history of the regular army of 'Old Contemptibles' that first went to war in August 1914. That said, the visitor to the Aisne valley and the Chemin des Dames cannot help but be reminded of the French occupation of the area and in particular the offensives that took place in 1917. For the Frenchman, the Chemin des Dames is almost as hallowed as Verdun and, as such, battlefield visitors will constantly be reminded of this by the legion of monuments and sites closely associated with that period of French military history.

While the main events of the British campaign are recounted in this guide, a lack of space has made it impossible to include the actions of every British unit and battalion that took part in the fighting. The reader wishing for a wider appreciation of the campaign will find that the author's *Battle on the Aisne 1914 – the BEF and the Birth of the Western Front* offers a more complete account and analysis of the battle.

For the British, the First Battle of the Aisne occurred a mere seven weeks after war had been declared on 4 August 1914 and much of those initial weeks had been spent on the roads of Belgium and France, either in retreat or – after 5 September – advancing towards the Aisne.

Sir John French, commander-in-chief of British forces in 1914.

After the official declaration of war on 4 August, four infantry divisions and one cavalry division of the British Expeditionary Force (BEF) under the

General Sir Horace Smith-Dorrien, commanding II Corps on the Aisne.

Lieutenant General Sir Douglas Haig, commanding I Corps on the Aisne.

overall command of Sir John French, began its embarkation for France on 11 August, completing the task just nine days later. By 22 August – the eve of the Battle of Mons – the BEF was assembled in Belgium and in position on the left of the French Fifth Army. General Sir Horace Smith-Dorrien's II Corps lined the canal between Mons and Condé facing north while Lieutenant General Sir Douglas Haig's I Corps was posted along the Beaumont–Mons road facing northeast. To the west Major General Edmund Allenby's cavalry and units of 19 Brigade guarded the canal crossings as far as Condé. The battle along the canal at Mons on 23 August was the first major clash the BEF had with the German *First Army* commanded by General Alexander von Kluck, and the outcome was inevitable. Outnumbered and out-manoeuvred and with General Charles Lanrezac's French Fifth Army already retiring on his right flank, Sir John French had little recourse

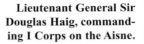

General Alexander von Kluck, commanding the German First Army.

but to retire. It was a retirement that took the BEF south of the Marne and first drew attention to Sir John's shortcomings as a commander-in chief.

The retreat from Mons, although considered to be a splendid feat of arms, was an episode the BEF emerged from by the skin of its teeth. It was not handled well by the staff at General Headquarters (GHQ), which was often conspicuous by its absence and notorious for the ambiguity of its operational orders. While there were numerous rearguard actions fought by the men of both Douglas Haig's I Corps and Smith-Dorrien's II Corps, it was II Corps that bore the brunt of the fighting at Mons and Le Cateau. Even so, during the Battle of the Marne and up until the Aisne valley was reached on 12 September, all units of the BEF were involved to some extent in fighting a series of seemingly unconnected and often frustrating engagements with German rearguard units. Such was the nature of the BEF's involvement in the Battle of the Marne that many in the BEF had no idea of the wider strategic picture. As Captain John Darling of the 20th Hussars (20/Hussars) remarked afterwards, 'it seemed curious to note that we never heard of this battle until it was over'.

To the eternal credit of the British soldier, the end of the retreat and the subsequent advance back over the Marne was seen as an opportunity to hit back at the enemy; tired and footsore they turned to pursue what they understood to be a thoroughly demoralized German army. Events on the Marne had seen a substantial gap open up between von Kluck's left wing and the right wing of von Bülow's *Second Army* and it was through this widening gap that the BEF was advancing towards the Aisne.

To the frustration of many, even after it became obvious that the German army was in full retreat, British staff officers – largely through their inexperience – handled the logistics of the advance badly. From GHQ there was little direction given to fighting units in the daily operational orders and even within divisions, staff officers failed to deliver effective movement orders or even prevent instances of friendly fire as divisional boundaries became blurred in the move north. The end result was predictable; the German army escaped and proceeded to withdraw in a relatively orderly fashion to the Aisne while the BEF struggled to pursue them in the torrential rain that made marching a purgatory

General Klaus von Bülow, commanding the German Second Army.

in itself. But even as late as the morning of 13 September, as German troops reassembled on the Chemin des Dames, the gap between their *First* and *Second Armies* still existed between the eastern village of Berry au Bac and Ostel in the west.

In those early weeks of the war the BEF was fighting very closely alongside its French allies and, given the size of the British force, it was a very minor player in the wider strategic picture that was unfolding across France and Belgium. To place the role of the BEF in perspective, by the time the British arrived on the Aisne the battle line stretched some 150 miles from Noyon in the west to Verdun in the east and it was only along a tiny fifteen mile sector in the middle that the British were engaged. (See Map 2)

But as British units became engaged all along the Aisne front, so the casualties mounted. Expecting to continue their pursuit of a retiring enemy, the British encountered a strongly held German line of defence. German shell fire proved to be remarkably accurate and powerful and it was some time before the British gunners could begin to mount an effective reply. The Aisne was certainly the beginning of the ascendancy of artillery as the major weapon of warfare but initially on the British side it was simply not up to the job in hand. Handicapped by the geography of the Aisne valley, British artillery was unable to provide the infantry with the firepower it required to take the Chemin des Dames or indeed fully support infantry attacks elsewhere along the

valley. But with the advent of aerial observation carried out by RFC pilots and the arrival of four batteries of rather ancient 6-inch howitzers of Boer War vintage, the balance began to swing more in favour of the British. The work of Lieutenants Lewis and James in developing the use of wireless transmissions from the air to artillery batteries on the ground was the start of a partnership that continued to develop through the war.

The lack of support from the guns of the artillery had profound effects on the infantry advance, particularly the units that had been engaged at Mons and Le Cateau. At Vailly, for example, the 3rd Division attack was doomed to failure as the much depleted battalions of Hubert Hamilton's division attempted to storm the heights of the

Lieutenant Baron Trevenen James, 4 Squadron RFC. Lieutenant Donald Swain Lewis, 4 Squadron RFC

Jouy spur. 8 Brigade, who had fought so doggedly at Mons on 23 August in the Nimy salient, had not a single machine gun between them on 14 September and had to rely solely on rifle fire. Similarly, on the Chivres spur, although the 5th Division were still in possession of some of their machine guns, they had left a significant proportion of their artillery behind at Le Cateau. On the right flank I Corps experienced similar difficulties as their advance ground to a halt on the Chemin des Dames.

In spite of these shortcomings the crossing of the Aisne River itself was a triumph for the men of the Royal Engineers, a feat of arms that is not often given due credit. The bridges the sappers constructed – often under fire from enemy infantry and artillery batteries – were indeed 'bridges over troubled waters', particularly as the river itself was swollen with rain and considerably higher than its usual September level.

British troops passing over a temporary bridge on the Marne built by 9/Field Company. It was bridges such as this one that were built over the Aisne.

It is a fitting tribute to the bravery and tenacity of the Sappers that one of their number, Captain William Johnston of 59/Field Company, was awarded the Victoria Cross for his gallantry on the river.

For the British the prospects of breaking through and taking the Chemin des Dames was never greater than on the morning of 13 September. Thanks to the Royal Engineers and the initiative of some brigade and battalion commanders, the passage of the Aisne had been achieved on both flanks and intelligence passed to Douglas Haig still indicated that the gap between von Kluck and von Bülow was

The château at La Fère-en-Tardenois used by Sir John French during the Aisne campaign. GHQ was situated some twenty miles from the Aisne, close to the RFC aerodrome at Saponay.

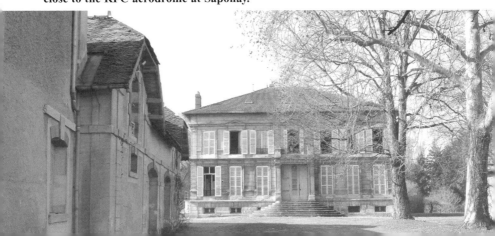

vulnerable. The opportunity was lost owing to the failure of GHQ to fully appreciate the situation ahead of them, a situation which by the evening of 13 September had completely changed. German reinforcements were known to have arrived and were entrenching on the Chemin des Dames, yet there was no further directive from GHQ other than to continue the pursuit. As a result divisions blundered into the battle piecemeal and without adequate artillery support and out of their failure grew the trench lines of the Western Front.

Despite the lack of progress and the hoped for continuation of the advance, the BEF and its allies did frustrate any intentions the Germans may have had in launching a new offensive from the Aisne in 1914 and precipitated the so-called 'race to the sea' as each opposing side attempted to outflank the other. Despite the superiority of German fire power, the BEF were steadfast in defence and were an even match for the German infantryman, but there is no doubt that the Battle of the Aisne in 1914 was an opportunity missed for both the British and the French.

The Chemin des Dames and the Aisne Valley

The Chemin des Dames ridge forms a narrow hog's back feature between the Aisne and Ailette river valleys. Running along the crest is the D18 that links the N2 in the west to the D1044 in the east, a distance of some nineteen miles.

As to who the 'dames' of the Chemin des Dames actually were is still the subject of debate amongst historians. Prevailing opinion suggest the ladies were Victoire and Adelaide, the daughters of Louis XV, who used the road to visit Madame Françoise de Châlus, a former mistress of their father who lived at the Château de Boves, near Vauclair, on the far side of the Ailette. It appears that in 1780 the road

The Chemin des Dames.

along the ridge was paved over in order to make the passage of their carriage a little easier. Remains of the original sandstone blocks can still be seen near Bouconville. However, some historians have suggested that the road that ran along the ridge may have taken its name from the 'Dames de Proisy' who, like Joan of Arc, accompanied Charles VII on his pilgrimage to the Priory of Saint-Marcoul de Corbeny the day after his consecration as King of France in 1429.

Early battles

Whatever the origins of its name, the Chemin des Dames is steeped in the history of conflict. As early as 57 BC Julius Caesar fought the Gaulois on the Chemin des Dames near Berry-au-Bac, where it is said over 100,000 Gaulois fought the legions of Rome in a battle that resulted in Julius Caesar's first victory in his campaign to defeat the Belgic alliance of tribes. The strategic importance of the ridge was underlined in 1814 when Napoleon Bonaparte fought the Battle of Craonne on the Chemin des Dames on his way to confront the Prussian General Gebhard von Blücher. Following his disastrous retreat from Moscow and defeat in Central Europe, Napoleon's Grand Army had still not fully recovered from the huge losses sustained in almost continuous campaigning. Taking advantage of a weakened French army, a strong Prussian-led coalition army under Blücher advanced towards Paris, reaching Soissons on 4 March. Napoleon gathered his army, comprising of largely inexperienced recruits – dubbed 'Marie-Louise' after Napoleon's second wife, because so many of them were too young to grow beards, and marched to meet the threat.

The statue of Napoleon Bonaparte on the Chemin des Dames.

At daybreak Napoleon found himself confronting the 24,000 troops led by the Russian General Woronzov. Much of the fighting centred around Hurtebise Farm, one of the key positions on the hillside, situated at the junction with the D886, east of the *Musée de la Caverne du Dragon*. The farm changed hands several times during the battle and was the scene of some desperate fighting led by the indomitable Marshal Ney. Despite the freezing temperatures the young inexperienced recruits still managed to climb onto the ridge in the face of the Russian guns only to be cut down in their hundreds. With the battle in the balance the day was saved by the arrival of the Garde in the early afternoon and the French managed to push the Russian and Prussian army back to the Soissons road, with both sides claiming a victory. Napoleon spent that night at Braye-en-Laonnois in the very house that von Blücher had occupied the previous evening. A

French victory it may have been but it was only a prelude to the Battle of Laon, which two days later resulted in a defeat and the beginning of the end for Napoleon and the First Empire. Today the last battlefield victory that Napoleon would preside over is marked by a statue of the Emperor on a small mound on the south side of the road between Hurtebise and Craonne, a point from which he observed the battle.

Hurtebise Farm still has two cannon balls decorating the gateposts and the monument to the young French infantrymen is close to the car park of the *Musée de la Caverne du Dragon*. At Pontavert is a half buried Russian cannon used in the battle and which can be seen at the corner of Rue Neuve Saint-Medard and Grand Rue.

General Robert Nivelle.

The Great War
During the Great War there were three battles on the Aisne and the focus on each occasion was once again the Chemin des Dames ridge. The 1914 Battle of the Aisne came about as a direct result of the German retirement from the Battle of the Marne, which took place further south as the huge conscript armies of France and Germany jostled for position almost within sight of Paris. In September and October 1914 the German army held onto its positions along the Chemin des Dames and although the French gained some ground during the Nivelle Offensive of April 1917 the French lost heavily in both casualties and morale. In the first week's fighting alone the French army suffered 96,000 casualties, of whom over 15,000 were killed.

General Henri Philippe Pétain.

It was the failure of the Nivelle offensive which precipitated widespread mutinies and acts of disobedience amongst units of the French army over the summer of 1917 and saw General Philippe Pétain – the hero of Verdun – replacing the disgraced Nivelle as commander-in-chief.

It was not until October 1917 – under Pétain's leadership – that the Chemin des Dames ridge west of Cerny was taken in the Battle of La Malmaison.

On 31 October 1917 the Germans abandoned their positions on the Chemin des Dames to fall back on a new line of defence north of the river Ailette.

By early 1918 the first men of the American Expeditionary Force had arrived in the form of twelve battalions of the 26th Division and were brigaded with French troops in a mentoring role. Spread across a front of thirty kilometres they held the front line between the ruined towns of Chavignon and Pinon with their reserves based in the St. Blaise Quarry at Nanteuil and the Froidmont quarries west of Braye-en-Laonois.

However, any territorial gains made by the French in 1917 were short-lived when their efforts were reversed in the German Blücher-Yorck Spring Offensive that began on 27 May 1918, when many of the British regiments that had struggled on the Chemin des Dames in 1914 were represented again by the legions of fresh faced youngsters in the ranks of IX Corps. On this occasion the British were further east, between Bermicourt and Bouconville, northwest of Reims, and under the command of the French Sixth Army. The French and British were dramatically pushed back to the Marne before the German offensive finally ran out of steam in early June.

The Second World War
Fighting returned to the Chemin des Dames in late May and June 1940 when another German army assaulted French positions along the Aisne. With the BEF now evacuating the French mainland at Dunkirk and other Channel ports, General Maxime Weygand pinned his hopes for a last-ditch resistance of the German Blitzkrieg on a defensive line that ran from the channel coast along the line of the Somme and Aisne rivers to join the Maginot Line at Montmédy – the so-called Weygand Line.

But Weygand's defences lacked depth and broke almost immediately; his forces, outnumbered and outgunned, fought in some instances to the last man, inflicting some crippling tank losses on the advancing German armoured divisions. But the end was in sight. On 9 June von Rundstedt's Army Group A attacked along the Aisne with four armoured and two motorized infantry divisions and

German Panzers crossing the Aisne in June 1940.

despite the gallant stand made by the French 14th Division, under the command of General Jean de Lattre de Tassigny, smashed through the French forces and headed for Paris. The fall of France had taken just six weeks. The battlefield visitor will find numerous memorials to the French troops involved in the 1940 fighting along the length of the

Chemin des Dames, such as the plaque on the wall at Hurtebise Farm commemorating the passage of the 4th Armoured Division, commanded by de Gaulle, and the memorial to the 99th Regiment of Alpine Infantry above Braye-en-Laonnois.

The final battle to be played out on the Chemin des Dames came in 1944 with the advance of allied forces after the landings in Normandy; many of the Germans who fell during this time are buried at the German cemetery at La Malmaison on the western end of the D18.

To this day some French historians feel that the sombre German cemetery marks a symbolic but ultimate occupation of the Chemin des Dames by a German army. The remains of the old fortress of Malmaison lie directly behind the cemetery.

The German cemetery at Malmaison.

The Aisne Valley

The geography of the Aisne river valley is characterized by a wide flat bottomed valley enclosed on both sides by high ground. The northern rim – the Chemin des Dames – rises to 199 metres at the *Ferme de*

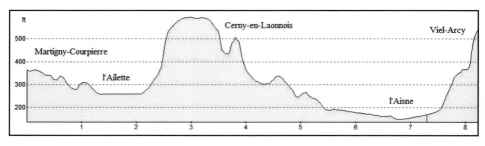

An exaggerated cross section across the Ailette and Aisne valleys from Martigny-Courpierre to Cerny-en-Laonnois on the Chemin des Dames and across to Viel-Arcy on the southern heights above Pont-Arcy, a distance of just over eight miles. The wide river valley of the Aisne is completely overlooked by the Chemin des Dames. In 1914 the BEF were faced with having to cross the river and scale the northern spurs to reach the German positions on the Chemin des Dames.

18

Poteau d'Ailles, while the southern heights are on average some fifty metres lower.

The cross-section makes it quite clear why the Chemin des Dames occupied such an important strategic position and just why the BEF were immediately caught on the back-foot when it was realized that the Germans had decided to stand and fight. Thus, when Major John Mowbray, the Brigade Major of the 2nd Divisional Artillery, reached the Aisne valley with the BEF in September 1914 he and many others had no illusions about the difficulties the British faced if the Germans were to hold onto the Chemin des Dames. He recorded his first impressions after crossing the Aisne at Bourg-et-Comin:

The country on both sides of the river between Soissons and Craonne consists of high ground some 250 – 300 feet [sic] *above the valley bottom. The direction of the Aisne is east to west – the main valley being about one mile in width. The valley bottoms are partly wooded and the slopes are almost entirely wooded with dense copses in which progress is difficult. One notable feature is a layer of limestone running at a height of about 200 feet above the valley which had been drawn upon for building stone resulting in numerous quarries and natural caves. The Aisne is about the size of the Thames at Oxford and unfordable. A feature is the canal running along the valley with a branch to the Oise at Bourg, passing the ridge north of the Aisne through a tunnel. The canal is also an unfordable obstacle. The watershed between the valley and the country further north is a continuous ridge of about 300 feet* [sic] *above the valley stretching from Soissons to Craonne along which runs the Chemin de Dames. From this ridge the plateau extends down in fingers.*

The fingers that John Mowbray referred to in his account are a series of spurs projecting south towards the river from the Chemin des Dames ridge. In the British sector nine spurs of varying size created ridges of high ground that led down towards the river and, as Mowbray's professional eye was quick to realize, it was these rounded spurs and re-entrants that dominated the fifteen mile long British front that were the key to gaining the Chemin des Dames ridge in 1914. His diary betrays his concerns as to the difficulties this valley would pose should the Germans decide to make a stand on the northern heights along the Chemin des Dames. In estimating the distance between the two ridges on either side of the valley as about six miles, he recognized that, 'any point in the valley can be observed from the Chemin de Dames ridge, as can most of the spurs and valleys and be very exposed to artillery

19

fire. The whole position on the river lends itself to artillery fire from the northern side'. Not only that, but he correctly weighed up the difficulties infantry and artillery would have advancing up the numerous spurs and side valleys, 'all of these positions', he felt, 'were exposed to cross fire and are tenable only with great difficulty'.

As also noted by John Mowbray, a feature of the valley is the layer of limestone that manifests itself in numerous caves and quarries. Although the area abounds with examples of these *creuttes*, only one – the *Musée de la Caverne du Dragon* – is officially open to the public. Over the centuries these *creuttes* have not only been used as a source of building material but in time of war they have been used by the population as refuge for themselves and their livestock. Many of the

The Cys-la-Commune railway station before the war.

The disused railway station at Pont-Arcy on the D925.

caves were used during the Great War by troops on both sides as shelter from shellfire and the weather and those at Paissy and Pargnan in particular feature amongst British accounts of the fighting in September and October 1914.

In 1914 a narrow gauge railway line ran north of the river from Soissons in the west to a point east of Vailly where it crossed the river and continued on the southern bank towards Rheims. A spur continued along the north bank towards Guigincourt and today there are still scattered relics of the railway to be seen, including the former station building at Pont-Arcy, which has been converted into a private house.

The destruction of the Aisne communities over the course of the Great War was almost total and the railway, along with its infrastructure, was completely destroyed. So great was the devastation that six village communities situated on or close to the Chemin des Dames were not rebuilt. These communities were so badly damaged that the decision was taken in September 1923 not to reconstruct them; and numbered amongst these were Ailles, Beaulne-et-Chivy, Courtecon and Vendresse-et-Troyon. However, their names do live on today in the names of communes to which they were attached, thus we have Pancy-Courtecon, Chermizy-Ailles, Vendresse-Beaulne and Moussy-Verneuil as a permanent reminder of the past.

The British Front Line in 1914
There were no trench maps produced by the British for the 1914 Aisne campaign and the precise location of the British front line can only be gleaned from the various battalion war diaries and the Official History. It is worth noting that some locations can be approximately pinpointed from early French trench maps produced after they took over the British sector in October 1914. Looking from left to right, the British front line began on the right of the French Sixth Army, with III Corps sector running from Point 151, just west of Bucy-le-Long to La Montagne Farm, where it continued southeast, running just south of Chivres to include the Missy bridgehead held by units of II Corps. Between Missy and the Vailly-sur-Aisne salient – a gap of just over three miles – was the German held Chivres spur, which extended down to the bridge at Condé-sur-Aisne and included the village of Celles-sur-Aisne. I Corps' sector ran from the eastern edge of the Vailly salient northeast to Cour de Soupir Farm, where it crossed the Braye valley, then traversed the southern end of the Beaulne spur from where it continued northeast – just south of Chivy – to Mont Faucon. Here the line passed south of the Sucrerie at Cerny-en-Laonnois before holding the edge of the Chemin des Dames to a point close to the Poteau d'Ailles crossroads where it

joined the left of the French Fifth Army. On the river itself, between Vénizel and Bourg, there were a total of seven road bridges, an aqueduct carrying the Oise-Aisne Canal over the river at Bourg, and a light railway bridge just east of Vailly. All the bridges – with the exception of Condé – were destroyed or badly damaged by the retiring Germans.

THE AISNE BATTLEFIELD, SEPTEMBER, 1914.

Map1. BEF positions on the Aisne as depicted in the official history of the Great War.

Chapter One

THE GERMAN ARMY ON THE
CHEMIN DES DAMES

AFTER THE BATTLE OF THE MARNE British and French forces were convinced the German army was in full retreat and, reckoned Christopher Baker-Carr, 'had shot his bolt and we had him on the run'. Baker-Carr was a former officer of the Rifle Brigade who retired as a captain in 1906. On the outbreak of war in 1914 he went to France with the BEF as one of the twenty five civilian volunteer drivers with the Royal Automobile Club Volunteer Force whose task it was to chauffer senior officers of the staff around the front. One of those senior officers, General Horace Smith-Dorrien, did not completely share his optimism:

> *The roads are littered and the* [German] *retreat is hurried; but I still realize that the main bodies of the German Corps in front of us may be in perfect order and that the people we are engaged with are strong rearguards, who are sacrificing themselves to let their main bodies get far enough away for fresh operations against us.*

Such caution was justified as the debris of retreat masked the real story of the German retirement. The retreating German army may have left the Marne in haste but the BEF failed to catch them and only came into serious contact with the enemy rearguards sporadically as they moved north – sandwiched as they were between the French Sixth and Fifth Armies. Smith-Dorrien's caution was shared by other individuals in the BEF who had already come to the conclusion that if the German army could hold their position along the heights of the Aisne valley they would be in a very strong position to parry the blow that was

German forces on the Aisne in rudimentary trenches.

approaching and perhaps turn their defensive positions into a new offensive action.

By nightfall on 12 September the pursuit of the German army had effectively concluded; its units were across the Aisne and busy consolidating their positions north of the river. *Hauptmann* Walter Bloem's account confirms that the German *10 Infantry Brigade* crossed the Aisne on 12 September near Soissons and marched via Bucy-le-Long up the valley to Chivres. It is unlikely that Bloem and the *12/Brandenburg Grenadiers* had any inkling of the potentially serious nature of the yawning gap in the line that still existed between von Kluck and von Bülow's armies which was still only lightly defended by the two remaining formations of von der Marwitz's *II Cavalry Corps*. The *5th Cavalry Division* had already been detached to the *Third Army* and the *4th Cavalry Division* was on the right flank of the *First Army* northeast of Rethondes at Tracey le Mont. However, by nightfall on 12 September both the *2nd* and the *9th Cavalry Divisions* were in place north of the Chemin des Dames – the *2nd* at Filain and the *9th* at Chavignon – while the Jaeger battalions of von Richthofen's *1st Cavalry Corps* were in place and under the command of *III Corps* to the north of Condé and at Vailly.

To appreciate fully the extent of the troop movements required to reinforce the defences on the Chemin des Dames we must return briefly to the Battle of the Marne on 7 September, when von Bülow pulled back his right flank behind the Petit Morin River and in effect increased the gap between himself and von Kluck. The response from German Army High Command (OHL) was to order the German *XV Corps* and the *7th Cavalry Division* from the German left in Alsace to move immediately to the extreme right of the German advance in order to outflank the French Sixth Army, which was threatening von Kluck. Ordered to join them, and form the nucleus of a new German *Seventh Army* was the *VII Reserve Corps* under the command of *General der Infanterie* Hans von Zwehl. *VII Reserve Corps*, consisting of the *13th* and *14th Reserve Infantry Divisions,* had been laying siege to Maubeuge which surrendered on 7 September, allowing von Zwehl to march south to the Chemin des Dames.

General Hans von Zwehl, commanding VII Reserve Corps.

Von Zwehl's Corps reached Laon at 6am on the morning of 13

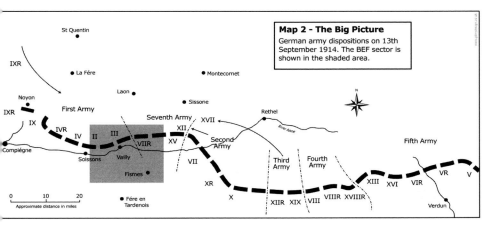

September, rested for three hours – during which time its commander was appraised of the situation on the Aisne – and then completed the final twelve miles to the Chemin des Dames. Over the course of 13 September Von Zwehl's men had marched over forty miles and temporarily lost some twenty five percent of its strength to fatigue.

OHL had placed von Bülow in overall command of the *First* and *Second Armies* as well as the *Seventh*; his orders were for *VII Reserve Corps* to move with all speed into the gap on the left of the *First Army*. Leaving Laon, von Zwehl's Corps moved southwest towards Chavonne, the *13th Reserve Infantry Division* deployed towards Braye and the *14th Reserve Infantry Division* to Cerny. A snapshot of the anxiety that was still prevalent at von Bülow's HQ is captured by yet another change of orders issued at 11am on 13 September, ordering *VII Reserve Corps* to Berry-au-Bac, where the right of von Bülow's *Second Army* was being threatened by the French. Unfortunately for the British it was an order that von Zwehl chose to ignore. As far as he was concerned his troops were far too committed to change direction.

By 2pm the majority of the *13th Reserve Infantry Division* was in position along the Chemin des Dames northeast of Braye. That afternoon *25 Landwehr Brigade* – which, according to General Maximilian von Poseck, the *2nd Cavalry Division* had 'picked up retiring from the direction of Bourg' – joined them along with 1,2000 reinforcements that had been intended for the *Second Army's X Corps* and a horse artillery *Abteilung* from the *9th Cavalry Division*. Thus by the afternoon of 13 September the crisis on the Aisne was practically over for the German army. Moreover, on the same day Belgian operations from Antwerp had come to an end with the Belgian Field Army retiring back within the defences of the city, which in effect released Berthold von Deimling's *XV* and Max von Boehm's *IX Reserve Corps* for immediate duty on the Aisne.

British intelligence on 13 September suggested the gap had not been substantially reinforced and there was little in front of I Corps but a strong force of cavalry and five batteries entrenched on the Chemin des Dames. Up until lunchtime this estimate was essentially correct, which, together with the news that the French 35th Division had crossed the Aisne at Pontavert and Conneau's cavalry were already pressing the enemy at the eastern end of the Chemin des Dames, made the prospect of a break-through a realistic prospect to Douglas Haig at I Corps HQ.

But it was not to be. By 1pm on 13 September the advanced guard of Haig's I Corps – 2 Infantry Brigade – had reached the top of the spur north of Bourg, enabling patrols from C Squadron, 15/Hussars, to press on beyond Moulins and Vendresse and to reconnoitre towards the Chemin des Dames. Major Frederick Pilkington soon reported contact with the enemy in the form of 'large numbers north of Vendresse with artillery in position'. Later that afternoon an RFC reconnaissance flight sighted enemy columns north of Courtecon. This time there could be no

French infantry forming a firing line.

German infantry of 1914.

doubt that a fresh army corps was moving towards the Aisne and that substantial troop movements were taking place along the Chemin des Dames. Major Archibald 'Sally' Home was at Troyon on 13 September with 2 Cavalry Brigade and recalled seeing 'masses of German cavalry moving all along the skyline on the main Rheims-Soissons [sic] road, we watched them for about two or three hours and estimated them to be a strong division'. He does not put a time on these observations but they may very well have been units of the *2nd* and *9th* German *Cavalry Divisions*.

The war diary of I Corps for 14 September indicates that I Corps divisional commanders were aware that the German *Reserve Infantry Regiment 53* and *56* were in position in the 'Cerny-Troyon neighbourhood', together with two Landwehr regiments, but it would not be for some days before the complete picture of German forces opposing them on the Chemin des Dames became apparent.

What was not clear to the British at the time was the extent to which German units were being trawled from elsewhere and diverted to the Aisne in order to bolster the forces already engaged along the Chemin des Dames. Consequently it was the arrival of fresh German formations and units such as the mixed detachment from von Kirchbach's *XII Saxon Reserve Corps*, *50 Brigade* from the *Fourth Army's XVIII Corps* and the five battalions from von Deimling's *XV Corps* that would finally put an end to any hopes of a breakthrough.

The strength of German forces facing Smith-Dorrien's II Corps was never in doubt. Von Lochow's *III Corps* consisting of the *5th* and *6th Infantry Divisions* and *34 Brigade* from *IX Corps* with two field artillery brigades were firmly in position by last light on 13 September; while in front of the British 4th Division, the *3rd* and *4th Infantry Divisions* of von Linsingen's *II Corps*, supported by two artillery brigades, were in position above Bucy-le-Long. Overall this was still a formidable fighting force and despite the attrition of the previous weeks there were at least 100 – albeit under strength – German infantry battalions opposing the seventy-six tired and weakened infantry battalions of the BEF, a figure that includes the four brigades of the 6th Division which would not arrive until 19 September.

Map 3. A sketch map found in I Corps War Diary, depicting the German units known to be facing the BEF on the right flank.

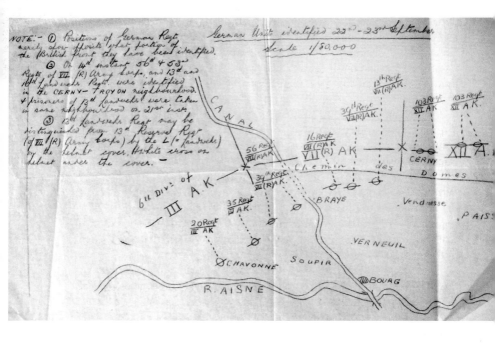

Chapter Two

THE 4TH DIVISION

THE FINAL MARCH OF 11 BRIGADE to the Aisne on 12 September began late that morning. Breakfast had been at 2.15am and although the initial orders had been for a 3.30am start, the four infantry battalions did not begin their march for another four hours. It was to be a very long and extremely wet day, culminating in the uncertain honour of being the first brigade of the BEF to cross the river at Vénizel and become established on the north bank. Commanding 11 Brigade was Brigadier General Aylmer Hunter-Weston, an interesting and somewhat unpredictable individual; commissioned into the Royal Engineers in 1884, he served in South Africa on the staff and later was in command of a unit of mounted engineers. Described as having 'reckless courage combined with technical skill and great coolness in emergency', the 11 Brigade Commander – known as 'Hunter-Bunter' by the men – was more usually seen on the back of a motorcycle, which appeared to be his preferred seat of command.

Brigadier General Aylmer Hunter-Weston, commanding 11 Infantry Brigade.

Lieutenant Gerald Whittuck of the 1/Somersets had a pretty good idea of what was in his brigade commander's mind as he approached the Aisne valley. 'Germans were evidently close in front of us as the inhabitants informed us that they had only passed through in the morning.' For Whittuck it was looking more and more likely that they would attempt the crossing of the river that night – an exercise he viewed with some apprehension. The young lieutenant was in temporary command of B Company, his diary recording they 'had three quarters of an hour's halt in the middle of the day, but otherwise were marching all day'.

The bridge at Vénizel had been badly damaged but, as Captain Francis Westland of 9/Field Company discovered sometime after 8pm on 12 September, only two of the demolition charges had gone off and, in his opinion, the bridge would take the weight of an infantry brigade providing they crossed in single file. This information was enough for Hunter-Weston. He ordered the whole brigade to begin crossing at once.

Lieutenant the Honourable Lionel Tennyson, a Hampshire and

The modern road bridge at Vénizel.

England cricketer and a grandson of the poet Alfred Lord Tennyson, also had memories of the march to Vénizel: 'After an awful march of twenty-seven miles still in torrents of rain to the village of Rozierés, we were ordered to advance once more just as we got ready to billet for the night, and arrived after yet another drenching at Vénizel.' Any thoughts Tennyson may have had of crossing the Aisne the next morning were dashed by orders for the brigade to cross the damaged bridge immediately and move onto the high ground above Bucy-le Long:

The whole of 11 Brigade crossed the river. This was the manner of their crossing, which at the time seemed to us the riskiest and most slap-dash proceeding ever ... In the midst of the inky darkness, and although the men were so tired with their march in the rain that they went to sleep as they stood or marched, they crossed the girder one by one. It was sixty feet above the river and quivered and shook all the time.

The Hon Lionel Tennyson in later life.

As advance guard, the 1/Hampshires were the first battalion to cross the Vénizel bridge. They were closely followed by the 1st Battalion Rifle Brigade (1/Rifle Brigade) and the stretcher bearers from 10/Field Ambulance, who reached the bridge at 11pm and completed their crossing in thirty minutes. Following the Rifle Brigade were the 1st Battalion East Lancashire Regiment (1/East Lancs) and Gerald Whittuck and the Somersets who 'crossed the Aisne just before light ... It was nervous work and took a long time as we could only go in single file'. The men, according to the Somerset's war diary, were tired and grumpy, but no mention was made of any opposition, as presumably the German rearguard had long since retired beyond Bucy-le-Long.

30

Hunter-Weston's own account of the night's operations describes the small arms ammunition carts being unloaded and passed over the girder by hand along with their contents. At Vénizel the river forms a wide loop which passes under the steep southern edge of the valley, allowing flat open water meadows to stretch for over a mile to the foot of the high ground. Across this open ground ran a single road – the present day N95 – which ran from the bridge to Bucy-le-Long, a road which was very much exposed to enemy observation and one which in the coming days would become almost impossible to negotiate safely in daylight. Above Bucy-le-Long the high ground took the form of three spurs where it was expected the enemy rearguard would be positioned.

Panoramic photograph taken the Royal Engineers in 1914 of La Montagne Farm and Bucy-le-Long.

Hunter-Weston expressed his concerns in his report to Division. He was quite aware as to the dangers of movement along the Bucy-le-Long road in daylight:

In order to hold the crossing of the river at Vénizel effectively it was in the opinion of the brigadier necessary to hold the heights above Bucy-le-Long which dominated the bridge and the flat ground between those heights and the river. He therefore ordered the brigade to advance to the attack of those heights and to seize them at the point of the bayonet. The leading battalion, the 1st Hants, were ordered to take the central spur on which is La Montagne Farm. The Somersets were ordered to the left spur, NW of Bucy and the Rifle Brigade the right spur north of Ste Marguerite. The E Lancs being kept in reserve south of the centre of Bucy-le-Long.

31

Dawn on 13 September

Captain Johnston and D Company of the Hampshires were the first British troops to enter Bucy-le-Long, which they found unoccupied as they passed through the deserted streets on their way uphill. As far as Gerald Whittuck was concerned, the march from the bridge was 'one of the worst night marches I remember'. After a march of thirty miles since starting off early on 12 September, the men were almost dead on their feet. The battalion, under the command of Major Charles Prowse, reached Bucy-le-Long just as it was getting light:

We were sent to occupy the high ground. This did not look much like an attack at dawn and I think it was just as well the ridge tops were not occupied, as the men were dead tired. We only saw a party of Uhlans on the top of the ridge as we reached the top and they disappeared at once. Prowse came up later and told me the points he particularly wanted me to guard and gave me direction in case of further advance. I posted groups to guard these points and withdrew my company to a bank running along the edge of a wood just below the crest of the ridge.

With 11 Brigade established along a frontage of three miles between le Moncel to Crouy, it was now the turn of 12 Brigade to cross the river. The temporary repair work on the road bridge was enough to allow three battalions to begin using the bridge at 6am on 13 September. The bridge had been passed fit for light duty after the sappers manhandled one of the 68/Battery guns across and by 11am the bulk of the brigade – together with the guns of 68/Battery – were over the river and moving under heavy shell fire across the water meadows towards Bucy-le-Long, leaving the 1st Battalion Inniskilling Fusiliers (1/Inniskillings) to bring the remaining guns and equipment of XIV and XXXVII Brigade over the bridge. From his vantage point on the Chivres spur, Walter Bloem had a grandstand view of the advance of 12 Brigade:

Stretched across the broad expanse of meadows between us and the river was a long line of dots wide apart, and looking through glasses one saw that these dots were infantry advancing, widely extended: English infantry too, unmistakable. A field battery on our left had spotted them, and we watched their shrapnel bursting over the advancing line. Soon a second line of dots emerged from the willows along the river bank, at least ten paces apart, and began to advance. More of our batteries came into action; but it was noticed that a shell, however well aimed, seldom killed more than one man, the lines being so well and widely extended ... our guns now fired like mad, but it did not stop the movement: a fifth and a sixth line came on, all with the same wide interval between men and the same distance apart. It was magnificently done.

Incredibly, in spite of the heavy shellfire from the German gunners, casualties were relatively light. Major Christopher Griffin commanding the Lancashire Fusiliers put much of this down to good discipline and resolve:

> *The battalion advanced across the shell-swept plain to Bucy-le-Long in lines of half companies. This manoeuvre was admirably carried out, largely due to the excellent leading, and disregard of danger, of company officers; the lines moved forward as steadily as if on parade. The casualties, which were few, would have been increased four-fold if there had been any hanging back or hesitation in the advance.*

Meanwhile on the right of Gerald Whittuck and the Somersets, the Hampshires had taken up positions around La Montagne Farm to find the enemy strongly

Hauptmann Walter Bloem photographed later in the war with his son.

entrenched some 1500 yards in front of them, while to their right the Rifle Brigade were in place north of le Moncel. The arrival of 12 Infantry Brigade extended the British line on the right whereas further

Panoramic photograph taken by the Royal Engineers in 1914 showing the Chemin des Dames ridge. The village of Le Moncel is on the left and Missy-sur-Aisne on the right.

back, a little to the north of Vénizel, were elements of the XIV Brigade guns which, although exposed to the German gunners on the Chivres spur, had little choice but to stand their ground. Up at La Montagne Farm the 31 and 55/Heavy Battery were in place providing support to the French advance north of Soissons, while at le Moncel, Lieutenant Cecil Brereton and 68/Battery were in support of the Rifle Brigade:

> We were then ordered up to support the infantry at the top of the hill. Found the Rifle Brigade there. We brought a section into action and immediately got shelled like fury from two places. Went back and got another section on the right. Noise appalling and could not make my orders understood. First rounds from the right section hit the crest and by the time we had run these up it was getting dark. The shelling was by now quite furious and we were only 800 yards from the German infantry who turned machine guns onto us as well.

The Lancashire Fusiliers' advance was halted briefly at Bucy-le-Long before they moved to Ste Marguerite, from where they were ordered to attack the western edge of the Chivres Spur. The hoped for assistance from 14 Brigade, who were in position half a mile west of Missy, unfortunately did not materialize in time to take part in the attack. Accordingly a rather piecemeal and under strength attack on the Chivres spur advanced either side of the minor road leading from Ste Marguerite to Chivres, with the 2/Essex on the left and the Lancashire Fusiliers on the right. The Essex war diarist recorded that the 'Lancashire Fusiliers were ordered to attack Chivres covered by fire from the battalion. The attack failed.' Major Griffin's account again:

> None of us realized we were about to bump into the enemy, well entrenched and in carefully selected positions ... the task assigned to us was to advance with the Ste Marguerite-Chivres road on our left, and attack the position east of Chivres. The battalion moved through the back gardens of Ste Marguerite almost to Missy, and entered the wood east of Ste Marguerite ... the Germans became aware of our presence, after we had advanced about three quarters of a mile, and opened a brisk fire on us.

All four of the Lancashire companies then came under heavy fire from enemy trenches south of the village and from the Chivres spur but continued to press on regardless until it became impossible to make any effective headway. The battalion reported sixteen killed, including four officers, forty-four wounded, including Major Griffin, and eighty three missing. The battalion diarist was quite clearly distressed by the number of men who were posted as missing:

Many under the heading of missing got to within 100 yards of the enemy, and whether killed or wounded, with the exception of 5 or 6 of the latter, who were brought in after dark, could not be recovered, and it can only be hoped that we shall meet the majority restored to health on our arrival at Berlin.

Apart from the optimistic reference to Berlin, the battalion had just experienced its first introduction of a frontal assault against well dug in infantry; and as it withdrew to consolidate the line and await the arrival of the relieving battalion, they had little idea that the line of hastily scraped rifle pits they occupied would soon stretch from the Belgian coast to the Swiss border. After dark the relief arrived in the form of 2/Manchesters from Brigadier General Stuart Rolt's 14 Brigade.

The 12 Brigade attack, undertaken without any significant artillery support and against a position of which they knew very little, made no progress in the face of enemy infantry and artillery fire. As 11 Brigade had already discovered, the British guns established on the heights south of the river were unable to locate and neutralize the German batteries on the high ground to the north of the river and in particular on the Chivres spur. Indeed Hunter-Weston had come to the conclusion early on 13 September that further progress was unlikely without considerable artillery support.

The war diaries of the other battalions who were in the line above Bucy-le-Long on 13 September recount a similar story of stalemate. The Rifle Brigade diary recorded the arrival of Cecil Brereton's 68/Battery guns and immediately sent one platoon from B Company to support the gunners, noting that once the battery opened fire, the enemy counter-battery fire was instantaneous, forcing Brereton and his men to retire with six men wounded and fifteen horses killed. Ordered to attack late in the afternoon, the Rifle Brigade advanced with two companies to the crest of the spur, where they were met with a withering fire from artillery and German infantry. Tennyson's diary:

About 30 of our fellows were killed and another 70 or 80 wounded, as well as Captains Nugent, Harrison and Riley, the last named very slightly. Sergeant Dorey, my old platoon sergeant of No 7 Platoon, when I was in B Company, was killed, and Rfmn Spindler and many others I knew killed. Sergeant Walker, who had done so well at Ligny and had been recommended for the DCM and Médaille Militaire, had his leg almost blown off in this advance, but hanging by a bit of bone. It is hardly credible but he took his pocket knife out and on the field where he lay, cut his leg off, and bound his leg up and when it grew dark he was still conscious when he was brought in on a stretcher.

The Rifle Brigade casualties were – according to the war diary – fourteen killed and three officers and thirty three other ranks wounded, Tennyson's estimate of the number killed and wounded being a little overstated. The 68/Battery guns were withdrawn under the cover of darkness:

> We went down the hill to Ste Marguerite and were told to entrench ourselves back by the Aisne. Major Short suggested we should take up a good position south of the Aisne, but for reasons of 'morale' this was not allowed ... looked at our position and then said to Loch i, "what a terrible place to put up, we will catch it alright tomorrow".

The Somersets were shelled heavily during the afternoon, losing three men killed and a number wounded, prompting Gerald Whittuck to begin digging the company in with their entrenching tools.

> We were holding a wide extent of front and it did not seem probable to me that we could remain in such a position. We were all expecting a further advance.

Like Whittuck, Brigadier General Haldane and 10 Brigade were also expecting to advance although, by the time he and his brigade were over the river, an element of doubt was apparent in his diary. 'It was uncertain at this time if the enemy intended to stand or continue his retreat.' Haldane's advance over the river had suffered a minor setback when the pontoon bridge put across the river by 9/Field Company was damaged on the night of 13 September. A complete 18-pounder field gun and limber drove over the side into the river, damaging the bridge and rendering it unserviceable for two hours.

14 September

The damaged bridge diverted Aylmer Haldane's Brigade back to the road bridge, where they too had to cross in single file over the creaking girder. 'We did not begin to cross till nearly midnight,' recounted Haldane, 'and reached Bucy about 1am on the 14th.' Haldane's arrival – almost twenty four hours after 11 Brigade first entered Bucy-le-Long – at least plugged the gaps in the 11 Brigade frontage that was worrying Gerald Whittuck but was far too late to make a difference against a strongly entrenched enemy.

Undeterred by the inconsistent artillery support, the 4th Division was ordered to push on north over the plateau between Vregny and Crouy with the intention of supporting the advance of the 5th Division from their bridgehead at Missy and dislodging the German guns at Clamecy, which were effectively holding up the advance of Maunoury's Sixth Army on the left. But without a significant increase in the level

The church at Bucy-le-Long shortly after the arrival of the 4th Division. Note the damage to the roof.

of artillery support and unless the French Sixth Army and the 5th Division on the right could make a decisive move forward, the plan was doomed to failure. Little if any progress was made by the French and the 5th Division made no headway at all. Haldane's brigade – which was not involved in the attack – suffered badly from shellfire, losing over a hundred officers and men as they struggled to find shelter at Bucy.

15 September

There was little change in the situation on 15 September, the day was spent improving positions by digging and collecting barbed wire from the surrounding farms. Apart from the limited supplies carried by the field companies, there was no supply of essential digging equipment and barbed wire available. Most battalions had lost their shovels and other stores during the retreat and were now scouring the nearby countryside for replacements. The shovel had become a weapon of war! As far as Haldane was concerned the maintenance of the line on the high ground above Bucy-le-Long was first and foremost but at the back of his mind was always the logistics of a possible retreat to the river. His diary betrays this underlying concern:

> At first the suggestion that additional bridges should be provided ... was not favourably received in higher quarters ... A retreat, even if carried out at night, would have been a hazardous operation, rendered still more so by the possibility of finding the pontoon bridge at Vénizel destroyed by hostile shells. But before we left the Aisne several alternative means of crossing had been made.

Additional crossing points were also very much on the mind of 10/Field Ambulance, who had established a forward dressing station in the school house at Bucy-le-Long. Shortly after crossing with 11 Brigade, they were joined by Sergeant David Lloyd-Burch, who crossed the river using the pontoon bridge: 'the Germans had a commanding view of the river and the flat country from the hills in the distance. Two ambulance wagons were hit getting into Bucy.' Lloyd-Burch had highlighted what was to become a recurring problem for the ambulance units over the next three weeks: the constant shelling from German artillery batteries made the evacuation of the wounded an almost impossible task during the hours of daylight. All that could be done for the plight of the wounded was to make life as comfortable as possible until darkness and the arrival of the ambulance convoys. Evacuation was made even more demanding in the early stages of the campaign by the condition of the bridges that were not really capable of supporting wheeled traffic and the unavoidable congestion on the winding road which ran west-east between Bucy-le-Long and Ste Marguerite. However, once the road bridge at Vénizel had been repaired a footbridge was added just downstream, while on 20 September two more pontoon bridges were

built at Moulin des Roches and Missy that relieved the congestion.

With 10/Field Ambulance firmly installed at Bucy-le-Long, the school house became the main receiving centre for casualties on the 4th Division front, whilst the little church at Ste Marguerite, which stood on the north side of the main

The church at Ste Marguerite, used as a dressing station by 10 and 11/Field Ambulance.

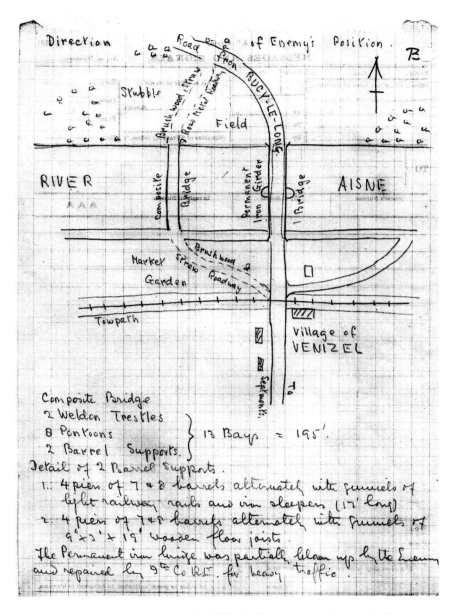

Map 4. A sketch map drawn by 17/Field Company, showing the bridge
at Vénizel and the pontoon bridge built downstream.

street, now acted as the main dressing station for all three infantry brigades.

Additional medical staff from 11/Field Ambulance eased the situation a little but the nature of the injuries – mainly from shellfire – was often extensive and put both staff and medical supplies under pressure. It was found, for instance, that the size of the 1914 issue field dressing was woefully inadequate when it came to dressing the wounds inflicted by the razor sharp splinters from high explosive shellfire. Not only that but the work of locating, dressing and evacuating the wounded from open ground was severely hampered by continuous shellfire and sniping by the enemy. For the RAMC it was just a taste of what was to become the norm for the next three years.

It was from Bucy that the precarious nightly evacuation of the wounded took place in the horse drawn ambulance wagons based at La Carrière l'Eveque Farm, just north of Septmonts. A mile further back, at the extensive Château Ecuiry near Rozières, the staff of Number 6 Clearing Hospital opened what was to become the centre for the evacuation of wounded from the left flank of the BEF. Yet the journey from Vénizel to Rozières by horse drawn ambulance was slow and tedious and for the badly wounded a painful and uncomfortable experience. Steep roads liberally covered with mud demanded a doubling of the number of horses required to pull each ambulance and the long suffering horse found this more arduous than the retreat. It was only the arrival of three motor ambulances on 17 September that eased the problem and reduced the journey time significantly.

Chapter Three

THE 5TH DIVISION

UNLIKE THE BRIDGE at Vénizel, the road bridge at Missy-sur-Aisne had been totally destroyed and the sappers of 59/Field Company were faced with a difficult task. Two of the three spans of the bridge had been demolished and the river was too deep to ford. At 3pm on 13 September Major Walker, commanding 59/Field Company, was contacted by Lieutenant Colonel Arundel Martyn, commanding 1st Battalion Queen's Own Royal West Kents (1/RWK), who had arrived with the battalion the previous evening.

Martyn explained his battalion had been ordered to cross the bridge, which was believed to be intact by divisional staff, and attack at all costs. With the heavy bridging train still a day's march away, and faced with the urgency of getting troops across the river, there was little alternative but to try and get the infantry across the river using makeshift rafts. By 5pm the enemy rearguard had been driven off the damaged bridge by the West Kents and 59/Field Company began ferrying the men of 13 Brigade across the river, an operation that took most of the night to accomplish.

Colonel Arundel Martyn commanding the 1/ Queen's Own Royal West Kents.

It was at this hotly contested crossing of the river that Captain William Johnston and Lieutenant Robert Flint of 59/Field Company spent much of the next day under fire ferrying ammunition across one way and wounded the other. Walker's subsequent recommendations for gallantry awards resulted in a Victoria Cross for Johnston and the DSO for Flint.

At 11am on 13 September the sappers of 17/Field Company arrived further downstream at Moulin des Roches and began ferrying 14 Brigade across the river. Second Lieutenant Kenneth Godsell described the night's activity:

> *On reaching the river we discovered a boat on the far side and a Sapper of my section stripped, swam across, and fetched it back. It was*

Captain William Johnston VC.

41

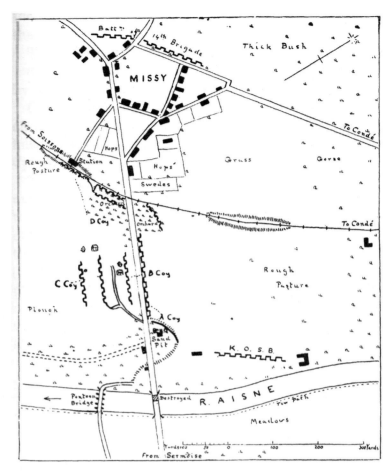

Map 5. Map from the 1/RWK history showing the Bridge at Missy and the positions of 1/RWK and the 2/KOSB around Missy village.

discovered later that there was nobody in front of us and the Germans were holding an entrenched position on the hills just the other side of Missy. By 12 o'clock No 2 Section had made a pontoon raft and had started ferrying the infantry across. We got 53 men on to the pontoon raft and nine in the boat. Each trip took 8 minutes if the party to board were ready on the bank. Later we constructed a landing bay each side by using the Weldon Trestles which accelerated boarding and reduced the time per trip to 6 minutes. The actual place of crossing was most convenient as it was where a track, which crossed the railway by a level crossing, ran into the tow path along the river bank. The point was sheltered from observation by a belt of trees and a small copse.

42

An artist's impression of Johnston and Flint ferrying wounded across the river in a makeshift raft.

Godsell estimated the 'river at this point was some seventy yards wide and flowed at a good rate'. But any hopes of a rest were soon dispelled when the advance guard of 15 Brigade arrived at 11.30pm. 'We found ourselves on the bank,' wrote Brigadier General Edward Gleichen, 'with a darker shadow splashing backwards and forwards over the river in our front, and some RE officers talking in whispers.' Godsell's diary records an exhausting night, with the last man of 15 Brigade crossing just before 6.30am the next morning. 'It was', he felt, 'a very wet night but we were too busy to notice it.'

Second Lieutenant Kenneth Godsell, 17/Field Company.

14 September

By dawn on 14 September both the Royal West Kents and 2/KOSB were across the Aisne and entrenched on the northern bank, taking up a position between the damaged bridge and the village of Missy. Captain Jim Pennyman recalled the crossing vividly and the scene that greeted him on the other side:

> The Engineers [59/Field Company] *had made a raft which had a nasty trick of sinking, and when we got there we found three* [half] *drowned men being brought round by Sergeant Major Fuller. For some reason, the Germans weren't opposing the crossing so the boat went back and forwards unmolested. I got leave to take my party across at once, as it would soon be light, and I thought we might be wanted. As soon as I landed I did a scout round on my own and found as follows: On our left the broken bridge, and a*

43

The road bridge at Missy looking across to the wooded area on the northern bank that was occupied by 2/KOSB.

road to the village of Missy. The village was half a mile off and, I think, in the hands of the Germans. Immediately to the right of the bridge was an old farm house with a depression behind it which afforded a certain amount of cover. All along the river bank was a thinnish wood thirty yards wide, sloping down to the river ... to our front we could see about half a mile of open park like country and then wooded hills, which we knew to be full of Germans.

At Missy, Captain Robert Dolbey, the KOSB medical officer, felt their position 'was a perilous one from a military sense.' The two 13 Brigade battalions were only in occupation of the Missy road and the wooded area on the north bank, 'both our flanks were in the air,' wrote Dolbey, 'we had no line of retreat save the damaged bridge, why we were not rushed we could never understand.' Pennyman agreed and felt the 'position was an extremely unpleasant one' and if it came to retirement they would have to swim for it.

Although the advance of the 5th Division ran parallel with that of the 4th Division on its left, they were separated by the Chivres

Captain James 'Jim' Pennyman, 2/KOSB.

spur on which the German *5th Infantry Division* were very securely entrenched. This promontory not only effectively separated the two British divisions physically but appeared to check any coordination of attack by them. From very early on in the battle it became apparent that the key to any advance on the left of the British front lay in possession of the spur. The high ground of the spur, with the old Fort de Condé on its summit, dominated the valleys on either side and while it remained in enemy hands any significant advance was unlikely to take place. Accordingly a two pronged attack was planned for 14 September: 14 Brigade would attack from the direction of Ste Marguerite and, when Missy was cleared of the enemy, 15 Brigade was to advance and attack the spur from the south east. Artillery support was in the shape of XV Brigade and the heavy howitzers of 37 and 61/Battery, all of which had been brought up to Bucy-le-Long.

The mist and rain which greeted dawn on 14 September did not prevent the German gunners on the spur from shelling the valleys on either side as soon as it was light and against this backdrop the 1/Duke of Cornwall's Light Infantry (1/DCLI) and the 1st Battalion East Surrey Regiment (1/East Surreys) advanced towards the wooded western slopes of the spur. The line of advance, described by the East Surrey's war diarist, was 'open and rather across the enemy's front and casualties commenced very soon', but by noon both battalions were in possession of the northern edge of Missy. It was a different story on the left of the DCLI, where the 2/Manchesters came under heavy fire from the direction of Chivres. The village was held by *52 Infantry Regiment* and against their dogged defence the British could make no further progress. The Manchesters had crossed the river the day before and been in action above Ste Marguerite in support of the 4th Division, relieving the Lancashire Fusiliers at dusk that evening. It was from their positions west of Chivres that they attempted to advance on 14 September, the war diary rather brusquely recording that they, 'took up a position of defence on the west of Chivres wood and remained there a week'.

Meanwhile 15 Infantry Brigade, who had crossed the river just before dawn on 14 September, courtesy of the Royal Engineers of 17/Field Company and their leaking rafts, made their way via Bucy-le-Long to Ste Marguerite, which was now held by 12 Brigade. With the 1st Battalion Dorsetshire Regiment (1/Dorsets) left in reserve in the shelter of the sunken road north of the village, the three remaining battalions of Gleichen's brigade moved on towards Missy, with orders to clear the Chivres spur from the south east and push on to Condé. It was, felt Edward Gleichen, 'rather a large order'.

Brigadier General Count Edward Gleichen, commanding 15 Infantry Brigade.

Even the process of actually getting to Missy along the winding road that skirted the high ground to the north was no easy matter:

The road thither was spattered with bullets and shells were bursting all along it. However, by dint of careful work we moved out bit by bit, cutting through gardens and avoiding the road, and taking advantage of a slight slope in the ground by which we could sneak to the far side of the little railway embankment that led to Missy station.

Gleichen met Brigadier General Stuart Rolt of 14 Brigade on the way and agreed to combine forces and attack the Chivres spur. One company of the Bedfords, together with another of the East Surreys, had already advanced some way up the wooded spur beyond the village where they consolidated their position and awaited the arrival of the main force. Gleichen's diary summarised the situation they were in:

The difficulty was that it was already getting late – 4.30pm – and that there was insufficient time for a thorough reconnaissance, thought we did what we could in that direction. However my orders from the divisional commander had been to take the ridge, and I tried to do it. I had got together three companies of the Norfolks, three of the Bedfords, two Cheshires (in reserve), two East Surreys (14 Brigade) and two Cornwalls (13 Brigade who had arrived via the broken bridge at Missy) – twelve companies altogether.

Although reconnaissance had established the presence of wire netting and wire entanglements in the woods, a number of battalion commanders were more concerned at the level of support available to the attacking infantry.

Lieutenant Colonel John Longley, the 47-year-old commanding officer of the East Surreys, was not entirely comfortable with the plan of attack; the battalion war diary recorded both his concerns and the subsequent advance:

It was not apparent to the commanding officer where the necessary support was to come from in his attack on the spur, and in his report on the situation he pointed this out ... The battalion crossed the entanglements unopposed, with the Norfolks on its right and the Bedfords on its left. After passing the wire it had a short steep climb before emerging on to a wide grass track leading up through the wood. The battalion was crossing this track with some of the Norfolks when a very heavy fire was opened on us from our right front, where on some rising ground was a German trench not 70 yards away. It was almost dark now which increased our difficulties, but the line of the track however was made good.

Lieutenant Colonel John Longley, commanding officer of the 1/East Surreys.

After conferring with the Norfolks and the leading company of the Bedfords, Longley was about to instigate a flanking attack when orders arrived from Gleichen to retire. This the Norfolks did immediately, leaving one company of Bedfords in support of the East Surreys. From Gleichen's diary it appears that a number of men were under the impression that they were being shelled by British artillery and had taken it upon themselves to retire; he also makes reference to groups of British infantry firing at their own men in the confusion of the wood. 'This may have been true', wrote Gleichen, 'for some shells were bursting over the wood; but whether they were English or German I do not know to this day.' There was undoubtedly some confusion of direction amongst some units in the gathering dusk which finally gave way to an equally confused retirement. The Cheshire regimental historian described the action:

Battalions on the left swung unconsciously to the right, and right in front of the Germans there was the most glorious jumble imaginable. Everyone blames everyone else and the Germans took full advantage of it all, as can be imagined. Men fell in every direction, whilst officers and NCOs strove, by word and whistle, to reduce this chaos to some sort of order.

While Missy was subjected to a furious bombardment, the stream of men retiring from the spur increased, leaving three companies of East Surreys and one of the Bedfords on the spur. On the spur Colonel John Longley redistributed his men and sent Lieutenant 'Monty' Montanaro forward with B Company, only to have him withdraw to the track again after he found the German line had been reinforced. Interestingly, there is an undercurrent of implied disapproval running through the East Surrey's war diary account of the action. Longley would have been quite justified in believing his position – albeit insecure and only fifty yards from the German trenches – was still manageable and with support could be held overnight. The orders from 14 Brigade to retire to Ste Marguerite must have bewildered him a little, particularly – as he correctly predicted – the attack would be continued the next day. Even more galling was the idea of the hard won ground upon which he was now standing being given up to an enemy who would spend the hours of darkness strengthening their positions. Reluctantly, Longley withdrew his men to Ste Marguerite as ordered.

13 Brigade at Missy Bridge

The original plan of attack for 14 September included the KOSB and the West Kents from 13 Brigade, who were in position north of the Missy bridge.

But any thoughts of advancing further towards the Chivres spur were

Map 6. Captain Jim Pennyman's sketch of the 2/KOSB positions at Missy Bridge.

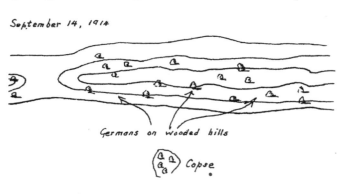

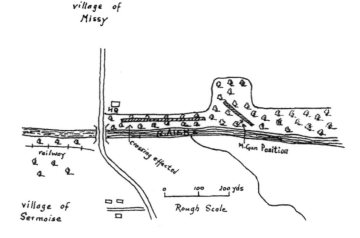

prevented by the volume of fire that effectively kept them pinned down on the north bank. Jim Pennyman's diary account describes the fight that was taking place along the wooded fringe on the right of the Missy bridge:

> *An increasing rifle fire was directed on to our wood, but no shell fire. The task allotted to the Borderers was to line out in the wood in order to prevent the Germans from sneaking down to the river bank, rushing the wood and taking in the rear the troops on our left front. Our front line had its right on the river and its left about the middle of the little salient wood.*

Aware that the enemy were indeed intending to attack their right flank, Pennyman, who was commanding D Company in the wood, deployed Second Lieutenant Gilbert Amos with his platoon to prevent any enemy intentions in this direction.

> *The bullets kept plumping in here in the most alarming manner, but we daren't leave it unoccupied. After about a quarter-of-an-hour the message came down from Amos to say he had already had five casualties. So we withdrew his platoon into the middle of the salient and bent our own left flank to join up with them. This seemed to be successful.*

With mounting casualties in the wood, Captain Robert Dolbey decided his presence was required on the firing line, accordingly he took whatever medical supplies he had to hand and crossed the river to establish his dressing station. It was a journey fraught with danger that began in a leaking raft:

> *A climb up the bank; a rush across the road; a swift tumble down the other side, and we were in the wood; a wood that seemed alive with death. How thankful I was that we had come in time; for there were wounded men everywhere and one didn't know where to begin. Then a corporal spoke to me and I turned aside to a little hollow; and there lay young Amos.*

Gilbert Amos died almost immediately he was hit. The 18-year-old former Wellington College schoolboy had only just joined the regiment from Sandhurst and was the

Captain Robert Dolbey, medical officer with the 2/KOSB.

youngest subaltern in the battalion. He had fought at Mons, Le Cateau and during the advance from the Marne. Mourning his death, Robert Dolbey was under no illusion that, 'life was very short for all the officers in this battalion; and if death had not come now, it would have surely have overtaken him in the next three months'.

German snipers up in the trees on the high ground to the right of the KOSB were exacting a heavy toll on the men. Pennyman himself had a close encounter with death shortly after Amos had been hit when a sniper's bullet 'went into the ground very close' to where he was firing a machine gun. But it was the second bullet that finally got him:

I thought it might be a sniper who had seen us, so we moved three of four yards to our right. The next thing I remember was a sensation like a blow with a cricket ball in the chest. It knocked me clean down, and I remember shouting as I fell bleeding profusely at the mouth. I felt quite certain I was a gonner, but managed to get up again and give some directions to the gunner, then I flopped down again.

Fortunately Robert Dolbey was on hand and his prompt action undoubtedly saved the young officer's life. 'Pennyman was brought in all limp and grey and cold; there was blood on his shirt in front and my orderly, seeing the position of the wound, said too loudly that he was gone ... but the age of miracles was not past.'

15 September

After the retirement from the Chivres spur the previous day, Gleichen was summoned to a riverside meeting with his divisional commander, Sir Charles Fergusson, at the Missy bridge. 'We got there eventually and crossed the river, sliding down steep slippery banks into a punt, ferried across, and up the other side.' Fergusson ordered a fresh assault on the spur led by the 1st Battalion Norfolk Regiment (1/Norfolks) with the Bedfords in support. On this occasion the attack was preceded by a thirty minute artillery barrage, which did little to suppress the enemy sniper fire that greeted the arrival of first light.

The Norfolks pushed on up the spur but soon came to a standstill in the wood where the German positions had been strengthened overnight. Ordered to advance up the valley to the east of the Missy-Vregny road, the 1/DCLI were soon under fire from the spur. Lieutenant Arthur Ackland described the valley as, 'a death trap, cross-fire from machine guns, infantry and artillery, no troops could have got further than ours, unsupported as we were from our artillery'. Such was the confusion brought about by the strength of the enemy defence that the rear battalions of 15 Brigade and the DCLI crowded into Missy, where the

The Rumpler Taube 'Dove', the German reconnaissance aircraft used to assist artillery batteries with targeting. The Taube was the first mass produced aircraft in Germany.

congestion was spotted from above by a German Taube with the inevitable result: at around 10am German artillery drenched the village with shellfire, forcing a temporary evacuation. The attack had been a total failure.

It was as Lieutenant Colonel John Longley had expected and it was not too long before he was ordered to move to Missy from the battalion's dugouts at Ste Marguerite to relieve 15 Brigade, who had retired to the northern edge of the village. The Surreys' war diary takes up the story, noting rather dryly that the 15 Brigade attack had 'apparently' not progressed very far:

> *The commanding officer called at Brigade Headquarters en route in order to arrange for some support from the two battalions of 13 Brigade who were still in position as yesterday S. E. of Missy, as it seemed to him one battalion only might be insufficient to hold the line previously held by a brigade ... the night was pitch dark with incessant rain so it was not to be wondered at that a searchlight from the German lines was much in evidence or that the posts of the 15 Brigade were in a hurry to be relieved. Hurry, however, on such a night was impossible.*

It was well past midnight before the last of 15 Brigade left Missy to cross the river via the new pontoon bridge erected by the 2/Bridging

An artist's impression of German forces using powerful searchlights to illuminate British and French positions below the Chemin des Dames.

Train at Vénizel. Gleichen recalls leaving the village during a heavy German artillery bombardment accompanied by 'German flare lights and searchlights', while John Longley observed rather sardonically that it had been 'a very trying night'.

Longley's request for support arrived on the evening of 16 September in the form of the 2nd Battalion Duke of Wellington's Regiment (2/Dukes), who were originally intended to be part of the attack on the Chivres spur but could not get into position owing to the weight of fire from the direction of Condé. The delay was on the river at the pontoon bridge built by 9/Field Company. Having repaired the bridge on 13 September, it was badly damaged again the next day by a French ammunition limber. Consequently the two waiting battalions of 13 Brigade were forced to take to the water in rafts. In the event it was only the Dukes who crossed the river that night; caught by the breaking dawn, the 2nd Battalion King's Own Yorkshire Light Infantry (2/KOYLI) found themselves trapped in the open and in full view of the enemy gunners.

Evacuation of the wounded

The arrangements for the wounded from Missy relied heavily upon the bridges at Missy and the winding road that led steeply up to the dressing station at Sermoise. Casualties for the 5th Division alone on the 13 September were sixteen officers and 728 other ranks killed and wounded; of these some eleven officers and 560 other ranks were wounded. As the majority of these men were in action on the north bank of the river, and the available bridges were in constant use by troops, it is not surprising that very few casualties reached Sermoise that evening. The next day enemy shellfire prevented to a great extent any movement by the field ambulances during daylight and it was only under the cover of darkness that 15/Field Ambulance was able to begin bringing out wounded men from Missy.

Even above the river, the road between Ciry and Serches was heavily shelled, disrupting movement between the dressing station and the divisional collecting station at Mont de Soissons Farm.

The 5th Division horse drawn ambulance trains suffered the same difficulties as their counterparts in the 4th Division; the steepness of the roads leading out of the river valley severely taxed the flagging strength of the horses and it was not until 20 September that motor ambulances put in an appearance to lighten the load.

A horse drawn ambulance of the type used on the Aisne.

Mont de Soissons Farm was the divisional collecting station for the wounded of II Corps. It was here that Jim Pennyman was taken after he was wounded.

As far as the Chivres spur was concerned it had become quite clear that its capture was beyond the current strength of the BEF. To the left and right of the British front the French were also in the same position and, as the 5th Division consolidated the line from Missy to Ste Marguerite, the battle entered a new phase.

Chapter Four

THE 3RD DIVISION

BETWEEN MISSY and the 3rd Division bridgehead at Vailly, the Condé salient drove a dangerous wedge through the British front. Originally allocated to the 5th Division as one of two crossing points over the river, the bridge at Condé was discovered to be intact on 12 September by a patrol of 4/Hussars led by Captain John Gatacre. A hail of fire from the northern end of the bridge greeted his patrol as they crossed over the River Vesle and headed towards the road bridge over the Aisne. At the time the approaches to the Condé bridge were said to be too exposed and the bridge too heavily defended to allow a direct infantry assault. From all accounts it would seem that this was never actually put to the test and the bridge remained in German hands for the whole of the British campaign.

At Vailly, Second Lieutenant Cyril Martin from 56/Field Company and Major Henderson, the officer commanding the 57th, soon discovered the bridge over the Canal Latéral was undamaged but the bridge over the river had a rather precarious looking single plank spanning a break in the superstructure.

The road bridge at Missy, taken in 1915. Note the remains of a pontoon bridge strewn along the banks.

Second Lieutenant Cyril Martin of 56/Field Company.

Despite making a wide detour to avoid being spotted by German infantry on the far bank, Henderson was hit in the elbow by enemy fire. Martin sent Henderson back 'with the man we had with us and then made a rough sketch of the bridge and went back to report'.

On returning to the bridge to see if the gap was safe enough to traverse by infantry, Martin managed to jump across and secure the plank. 'It was a pretty warm time as the Germans were firing from quite close.' The bridge, Martin felt, was probably not going to take the weight of an infantry brigade, but after a personal inspection by Hubert Hamilton, commanding the 3rd Division, 8 Brigade were ordered to cross the river using the bridge. It was a repeat of the Vénizel experience, a single plank spanned the breach in the road bridge and the Royal Irish and Royal Scots began crossing at 3pm on 13 September. Being daylight, they were under continual shell fire from German batteries, both battalions taking casualties. However, by 6pm they had established themselves around Vailly: the Royal Irish east of St. Pierre and the Scots at Vauxcelles Château, a mile or so northwest of Vailly. That night 9 Brigade followed on, using the same precarious plank, while 56 and 57/Field Companies began the task of erecting a pontoon bridge across the river, completing their task by 3am on 14 September.

The high ground north of Vailly is divided by the Jouy valley up which the D14 runs to join the N2. On the left of the D14 is the Jouy spur and on the right the larger Ostel spur with the St Précord spur running south from La Rouge Maison Farm.

Hamilton's plan of attack was to keep McCracken's 7 Infantry Brigade in reserve and deploy Doran's 8 Brigade to advance up the Jouy spur and Shaw's 9 Brigade to the Ostel spur, where it was hoped to join up with the left of the 2nd Division, advancing north from La Cour de Soupir Farm.

But even before 8 Infantry Brigade reached the river they came under fire from enemy batteries. Arriving at Chassemy, which overlooked the river below, German gunners were quick to greet them with a heavy barrage.

Despite the grey and wet start to the day, the single road – the D14

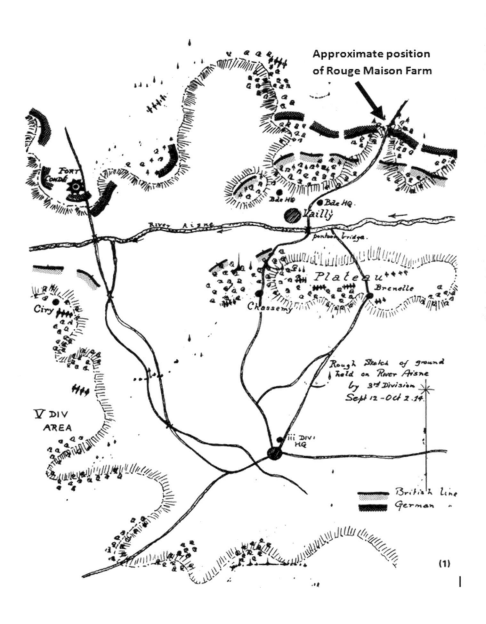

Map 7.   A sketch map drawn by Lieutenant Billy Congreve showing the positions of the 3rd Division around Vailly.

– that led down to the bridge at Vailly was clearly visible to the Germans on the Chivres spur and as the 2nd Battalion Royal Irish Regiment (2/Royal Irish) left the security of the wooded slopes they came under shell fire sometime after 8.15am. 26-year-old Lieutenant Frederick Rushton immediately ordered his men to take cover on either side of the road, noting that, 'a battery of our guns took up a position in [the] wood in rear of open space. Enemy shelling the edge of wood steadily. Range absolutely correct. Each shell overhead, bursting in rear.' The British battery seen by Rushton and his men was 49/Battery from XL Brigade, which had unlimbered, not in the wood, but in the open and commenced firing across the valley. All too soon it was silenced by the greater fire power of the German howitzer batteries, putting two guns out of action and forcing the gunners to abandon the guns, or as Frederick Rushton rather benevolently put it, 'our gunners have moved back, leaving [the] guns ready to fire when required'.

At 10am, under the cover of the guns of 48/Heavy Battery. which had come into action north of Brenelle, the 2nd Battalion Royal Scots (2/Royal Scots) began working their way downhill through the woods to the right of the road to reach the canal a little to the east of the bridge. They were followed by the Royal Irish and the 4th Battalion Middlesex Regiment (4/Middlesex), all of whom were successfully over the river and established on the other side by 4pm on 13 September. It is worth noting here that 8 Brigade were without the 1st Battalion Gordon Highlanders, who had suffered badly at Le Cateau on 26 August, losing over 700 officers and men killed or taken prisoner and in the process practically ceasing to exist as a battalion. It was only at the end of September that the battalion was at full strength again and rejoined the brigade.

14 September

After dark Shaw's 9 Infantry Brigade crossed the river, the 1st Battalion Lincolnshire Regiment (1/Lincolnshires) historian describing their passage, which took place in the pouring rain:

> It was near midnight before the Lincolnshire began their hazardous crossing. The advance was by sections, each section first crossing the bridge over the canal and then over the single plank spanning the gap in the broken bridge over the river in single file. A false step left or right would have meant certain death from drowning. Every now and then a bursting shell would throw the weird scene into prominence but not a single man was hit, neither did anyone fall into the river. Progress was very slow, but once across the men had to double several hundred yards to

Officers of the 1/Lincolnshire Regiment inspecting a German artillery piece captured by the battalion on the Marne.

where the battalion was forming. When the last man had joined, the battalion marched off through the town of Vailly at a rapid pace and wheeled right up a narrow lane and then across a large tract of cultivated land on to a high ridge to the south west of Rouge Maison Farm.

The crossing 'took the best part of two hours and we had a weary wait in the pitch darkness', wrote Captain Gerard Kempthorne, the medical officer attached to the battalion. As the battalion moved up above Vailly onto the southern slopes of the Ostel spur they found themselves in what Kempthorne described as a 'vast turnip field', where they found the 4th Battalion Royal Fusiliers (4/Royal Fusiliers) already in place, having completed their crossing by 11.30pm.

The Lincolns extended the line to the left of La Rouge Maison Farm and the medical officer and his team dug in behind the firing line alongside one of the A Company platoons:

We were in a trench with about 30 men, all cold, hungry, and shivering and caked with mud from head to foot. The ground rose a little, 100 yards in front of us, and all that was to be seen was wet turnips, on either side, and to the rear.

At dawn on 14 September two companies of the Royal Scots advanced up the Jouy spur through the mist and rain with the Royal Irish on their left and the Middlesex on the right. Artillery support, such as it was, provided little to assist the advance and, as the Royal Scots historian remarked, 'the German fire by this time was positively murderous'. The German trenches were on the reverse slope of the crest and as soon as the British troops came into range they were effectively stopped in their tracks by machine gun and artillery fire. Major Hamilton Finch, advancing with the Middlesex, was alarmed to find they were 'for a short period under fire from several directions' as German machine gun teams managed to establish a firing line on the British flanks. 'An effort was made by some to take their machine guns', wrote Finch, 'but it was a hopeless attempt and our men got back with wonderfully few casualties.' B Company of the Royal Irish found themselves involved in heavy fighting in the wooded slopes and, shortly after being reinforced by half of A Company, Lieutenant Frederick Rushton was killed at the head of his platoon. Pushed back, the Royal Irish took up a new position on the minor road running east of Vauxelles towards Vailly, with the Royal Scots and Middlesex on their left.

The lack of fire power offered by the attacking 8 Brigade would certainly have given encouragement to the German counter-attack, which was launched just before 9am. It was well timed and the British were in no position to respond effectively, although they did manage to hold on for close to an hour; long enough for the enemy attack to lose its momentum. At around 10am the brigade began to fall back. Major Finch's account:

> Now came the moment for us to retire, and this might have been a very unpleasant experience as the enemy's guns were very busily at work on the bend of the road we had to follow before we could get on the high ground. However, we reached another ridge with, I believe, no casualties, by doubling round the bend at about 20 paces interval. The order then came that we were to hold on there (on the north side of the river) at all costs; this was about 4pm.

The attack had little chance of success from the outset. On 14 September 8 Brigade had to rely very much on the fire power from its rifle companies, particularly as the three battalions had not a single machine gun available between them. Moreover, the combined manpower of the three battalions only numbered some 1500 officers and men, a state of affairs that can be traced directly to the brigade's action in the Nimy salient at Mons on 23 August and the subsequent encounters at Le Cateau and the Marne. At Nimy the Middlesex and the Royal Irish had fought a desperate rearguard action as they retired towards Cuesmes, both regiments losing heavily in the process. Le Cateau further depleted the brigade's ranks, with the loss of the Gordon Highlanders, as did the rigours of the retreat. It was only after the arrival of the 1st Battalion of the Devonshire Regiment (1/Devons) on 15 September that the brigade could put two machine guns in the firing line!

A British machine gun team near Rouge Maison Farm. These are men of the 1/Leicestershire Regiment. Note the absence of steel helmets which were not generally issued until 1916.

Little wonder then that the attack on the Jouy spur failed.

On the Ostel spur, at La Rouge Maison Farm, the morning mist had concealed the presence of the German positions, which were only 600 yards away just below the crest of the ridge. It was from these trenches that the German attack was launched at 7.30am. Somewhat taken aback by the ferocity of the supporting shell and machine gun fire, the appearance of waves of enemy infantry initially had the British on the back foot, prompting Brigadier General Shaw to reinforce the line with the Northumberland Fusiliers; these three battalions – although ordered to counter attack – were eventually pushed back almost to the edge of the spur. Throughout the morning the enemy continued the attack, wave after wave advancing against the British line. According to the Royal Fusiliers' war diary, they managed to hold their sector of the line for 'some time' until the regiment on the right gave way, forcing them to retire to a sunken road about 200 yards south of La Rouge Maison Farm. The regiment in question was 1/Lincolns, who were under attack from German machine gunners who had managed to get into La Rouge Maison Farm. The enemy were pouring heavy fire into A and C Companies in support of infantry who were attacking the Lincolns' right flank from the woods near Folemprise Farm. It was an unenviable position.

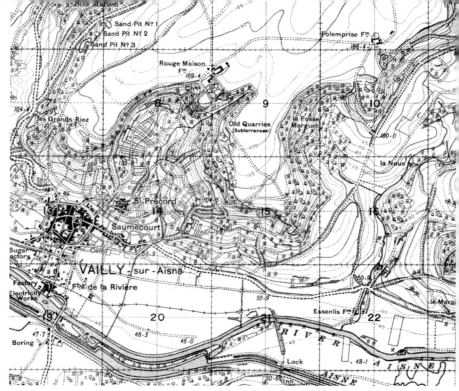

Map 8. The high ground above Vailly showing the position of Rouge Maison Farm. Note the light railway bridge to the east of Vailly used by John Lucy and the Royal Irish Rifles on 14 September.

Calling for support, four companies of Royal Scots Fusiliers – two companies to the right flank and two to the left – were ordered up to the firing line. Advancing through turnip fields on the right of the besieged Lincolns, the Scots came under heavy machine gun fire from the woods on their right flank which, without any supporting fire from British artillery, eventually forced Captain George Briggs to order a gradual withdrawal. Tragically, Briggs was killed during the retirement, along with seven other ranks, the battalion also recording sixty seven wounded and ninety missing. It had been a costly morning for the Scotsmen.

Exactly when the Lincolns retired is unclear. The battalion war diary covers the whole action in eight lines but does note seven officers and 184 other ranks killed, wounded or missing. Kempthorne's diary sheds some light on the story at the point the Lincolns began to pull back:

> *After a time it became obvious our flank was threatened as the bullets began to hit the traverses instead of the parapet and we had to pull our wounded under their protection. Then I saw a*

section of our men retiring ... but we hung on, and continued our work, till to my disgust I sighted the whole German line advancing over the skyline 200 yards away. It was obviously hopeless to make a bolt in the open over slippery turnips and still clay so we carried on. When they were about 50 yards off I climbed out of the trench brandishing a very dirty handkerchief and they made no attempt to fire on me. By this time the brigade must have made good their retreat down the line to the river, for all was quiet.

Simpson, in his history of the Lincolnshire Regiment, points outs the battalion not only retired to Vailly but continued over the river crossing by the light railway bridge! The situation had now become critical. With the retirement of the Lincolns, the right flank of 9 Infantry Brigade was now wide open, increasing the gap between them and the left of the 2nd Division on the spur above Soupir to a distance of one and a half miles. On top of everything else, the Guards Brigade at Cour de Soupir Farm, along with the Connaught Rangers, was under a furious attack that began at 10.30am and threatened to push the division back to the river. As far as the 3rd Division was concerned, the mist and fog that clung to the hillsides had rendered the artillery batteries on the southern heights of the river practically useless for a large part of the day and at this point in the battle there was a real possibility of a strong German counter attack splitting I Corps on the right flank from the remainder of the BEF. Hamilton was now in need of his reserves; but the only troops that were on the northern side of the river and available to plug the gap were 5 Cavalry Brigade, who had crossed early that morning and were now at Vailly. Infantry reserves in the form of McCracken's 7 Brigade were still in the process of crossing the river.

5 Cavalry Brigade

A degree of panic may have accompanied the orders sending the cavalry to Vailly to plug the gap in the line left by the Lincolns' retirement. When Captain John Darling, the signalling officer with the 20/Hussars, crossed with his regiment over the pontoon bridge, the Scots Greys and 12/Lancers had already arrived and dismounted at Vailly:

The whole valley, including the bridge, was under hostile observation and artillery fire. It was a misty morning, and to this alone could be attributed the fact we had got so far without drawing the enemy's fire. As the regiment reached the bridge the fog lifted, the German gunners spotted us and started firing. Pontoons are not intended to carry cavalry at a trot, at least this

A British cavalryman in October 1914, probably taken during the move to Flanders.

> *one was not, so the Colonel dismounted the regiment and gave*
> *the order to lead over in single file. This we did.*

As J Battery of the Royal Horse Artillery (RHA) prepared to cross the river to Vailly they were stopped by Brigadier General Chetwode about 400 yards short of the bridge. He explaining that 'the village of

A section of a Royal Horse Artillery unit. The photograph was taken in 1915 during a training exercise.

From a painting by George Rowlandson depicting Theodore Wright's death at the pontoon bridge at Vailly. Units of 5 Cavalry Brigade are crossing under shellfire.

Captain Theodore Wright VC.

Vailly was full of cavalry who could not get on as the infantry attack was held up'.

The battery retired and came into action east of the Chassemy road, about a mile from Vailly, where they opened fire rather ineffectually on a German battery.

Controlling the confusion of movement across the bridge on the morning of 14 September was Captain Theodore Wright, the 57/Field Company officer who had been awarded the Victoria Cross for his bravery at the Mariette Bridge during the Battle of Mons on 23 August. Wright and Lance Corporal Alfred Jarvis – also 57/Field Company – had both won the coveted cross for their work in blowing the canal bridges at Mons.

Tragically, controlling the movement of the cavalry across the pontoon bridge at Vailly was to be Theodore Wright's last act, as he was killed by shellfire whilst assisting wounded troopers to shelter. Wright may not have known about the award of his VC as it was not formally announced in the *London Gazette* until November 1914.

The 600 or so rifles that 5 Cavalry Brigade could have mustered were never called into action. The 12/Lancers merely mention that after being 'pushed across at Vailly' they were 'unable to debouch and had a most unpleasant return passage across the two canal bridges'. Quite why they were not deployed to shore up the line is anyone's guess – the Official History rather lamely explains they were not required as the situation had improved. The 20/Hussars did an immediate turn-about on reaching the village after being told they were not needed. John Darling again:

> *Once more we had to face the ordeal of leading over* [the bridge] *in single file under heavy shell fire. By now the Boche had got the range pretty well, and it became an unpleasant manoeuvre, especially for the last squadron, B. The marvel is that we did not lose more men. The total casualties in the regiment were only ten.*

One suspects that the infantry battalions of the 3rd Division that had been engaged that day above Vailly would have been only too glad to report ten casualties.

7 Infantry Brigade

Lieutenant Alexander Johnston, the signalling officer with Brigadier McCracken's 7 Brigade, was relieved somewhat by orders to cross further up the river, using the repaired light railway bridge, which took them away from the shrapnel torn crossing at Vailly.

This delay, however, almost certainly contributed to the difficulties

Lieutenant Alexander Johnston who was on 7 Brigade staff in 1914.

9 Brigade were experiencing on the spur. Even before McCracken's brigade had crossed over, elements of 9 Brigade were already seen to be withdrawing.

Corporal John Lucy reached the railway bridge at 3.30pm with C Company of the 2nd Battalion Royal Irish Rifles, just as the German shell fire increased:

We were making for the railway bridge east of Vailly, which at that moment was being recrossed by an English regiment retiring out of action from the northern side of the river ... As we approached the bridge we saw that it was completely wrecked ; a tangled mass of ironwork, most of which was submerged, with a dead horse held against it by the current, and only a line of single planks, which sagged in the middle, as a means of getting over.

Lucy felt the whole business of getting over the river was 'a nasty proposition', remarking angrily that a shrapnel bullet had penetrated his haversack and torn into a folded towel inside. Reforming, his battalion followed the 1st Battalion Wiltshire Regiment (1/Wilts) – who had crossed before them – up towards the St Précord spur and as the battalion moved steadily uphill and came within range of the enemy the casualties began to accumulate, 'a good many men were knocked out, but we did not miss them in the excitement'. The German riflemen, thought Lucy, were generally rotten shots:

Corporal John Lucy, 2/Royal Irish Rifles. The photograph was taken after he was commissioned.

Their rifles cracked sharply now, and the whistle and whine of bullets passing wide changed to the startling bangs of bullets just missing one. The near rattle of machine guns sent our hearts thumping ... Our own shells were bursting a short distance ahead, just beyond the crest line clearly visible to us. This line marked the near edge of a large plateau, and as we made it in a last rush we found this plateau edge forming a small continuous cliff of chalk giving good protection from bullets and fair cover from shell fire.

Twenty-four year old Lieutenant Gerald Lowry was a platoon commander in C Company of the Irish Rifles, who recalled the advance in his diary:

We had a splendid fight that day, taking the hill and the wood on its summit before evening. The position was at the Maison Rouge Farm ... our flank here swung round into a wood, and we lined a bank fronting a stubble field which led upward at a gentle slope.

The Irish Rifles had established themselves on the left of the Wiltshires and, as the remainder of 7 Brigade crossed the river, 8 Brigade fell back to the southern edge of the Jouy spur. Fortunately for the BEF the line was now relatively stable, there was no German counter attack and the British guns on the heights at Chassemy finally managed to get into action. 130/Battery fired some 200 rounds at enemy infantry on the Ostel spur and 48/Heavy Battery did have some success in silencing machine gun positions near Folemprise Farm. However, other artillery units, such as XL Brigade on the Brenelle plateau and XLII Brigade east of Chassemy, failed to come into action all day.

67

The fighting on the 14th was concluded with an unsuccessful night attack at 10pm on the British line, an attack of which Alexander Johnston was made aware by the rifle and machine gun fire that resounded 'all along the line for some time'. Overall it had been a frustratingly difficult day, a day that had begun in anticipation of a general advance and for the 3rd Division one that almost ended in disaster. As the rattling of rifle fire died away in the darkness, the line held by the division ran in a semi-circle around Vailly. The position was hardly a secure one, the gap between the 3rd and 2nd Divisions was only covered by outposts and there was still uncertainty as to the intentions of the Germans. Johnstone's diary entry for 14 September merely stated what most of his contemporaries were thinking, 'this is no rearguard action we are fighting now but I should say is part of a big attempt by the Germans to hold the line of the Aisne?'

15 September

Dawn on 15 September was again wet and cold. For the Royal Irish Rifles – established a little to the south of La Rouge Maison Farm – the morning began with a scouting patrol from D Company under the command of Lieutenant Charles Dawes. Lieutenant Colonel Wilkinson Bird was anxious to discover the exact whereabouts of the enemy and it was not long before Dawes' patrol found them situated just below the crest.

A sharp fire fight ensued during which one man

Lieutenant Colonel Wilkinson Bird, commanding 2/Royal Irish Rifles.

British infantry of 1/Leicestershire Regiment near Rouge Maison Farm.

was killed and Dawes and another wounded; they retired under fire. Not content with the outcome, and still unsure as to whether the enemy had retired or not, Bird ordered A and C Companies to advance. Gerald Lowry was with them:

> There was practically no cover, and the ground was hard and bare, so we proceeded by short rushes. The Germans were, however, waiting for us, and when we got to within a few hundred yards of their line they opened a perfect hail of machine-gun and rifle fire and shrapnel – a veritable tornado of flying, shrieking metal, well directed. Part of the company on our left got into the first line of German trenches, but were ultimately compelled to retire, as it was obvious that not only were the Germans dug in,

but were in full force. Captain Bowen-Colhurst, who commanded this reconnaissance, was badly wounded in the assault, whilst two officers were killed and half the men killed or wounded; the machine-gun and shrapnel played havoc amongst us as were getting back across the open valley.

The Lincolns returned to Vailly; after spending the night of 14 September in the village square they 'marched to the top of the hill again and were kept in support the whole of the day, and at dusk lay

The church of Notre-Dame at Vailly where Lieutenant Henry Robinson and 8/Field Ambulance attended the wounded.

alongside the road'. This was presumably the minor road that still runs north east from Vailly towards La Rouge Maison Farm.

Casualties from the fighting on the spurs above Vailly were brought down to the advanced dressing station established by 8/Field Ambulance in the twelfth century church which bordered the village square. The village had suffered a good deal from German shelling but fortunately it was only the lower end of it, near the river, that had borne the brunt of this so far. The northern end, which included the church, was still under the lee of the steep high ground of the Ostel spur behind. It was not until after 15 September that the church and the square were shelled. Lieutenant Henry Robinson's diary provides a detailed and rather distressing account of his stay in the village:

> *I, more or less, took charge of the church, though others used to come and assist whenever they had a spare moment ... The scene in that church was one that defies all description. It was a large church for the size of the town [sic], and the whole of the floor space was covered with mattresses; we even had to place them on the altar steps. Wounded men, covered in mud and blood, were everywhere, and space was so precious that we could not even keep gangways through the rows of mattresses. To get to our patients we had to step over others. Many of the wounds were very serious, and my bottle of morphia was in constant request, in fact it was soon empty and I got a fresh stock from a chemist in the town ... During the three nights I spent in Vailly I slept altogether about five hours. Fresh batches of wounded were coming in all hours of the day and night, and the work was absolutely incessant.*

As with the casualties at Bucy-le-Long, it was not until nightfall each evening that the wounded could be moved across the pontoon bridge and onto the ambulance trains waiting to transport them to Braine. Parties of stretcher bearers from 7 and 8/Field Ambulance were sent across the river each evening and all those wounded who were able to be moved were carried or assisted to walk down through the town and over the river. The Germans of course were well aware of this nocturnal evacuation and shelled the bridge on average every twenty minutes; this led to a deadly game of chance as the bearers waited for the interval between each shell to traverse the bridge. 'But if one happened to be going down with wounded to the bridge and no shell had come for a good many minutes', wrote Robinson, 'there was always a chance of catching one just as the bearers got to the bridge.'

Many of the casualties were the result of German shellfire, which subjected the troops to some quite horrific injuries, some of which

Henry Robinson and his colleague doctors knew instinctively to be fatal. In the early months of the war the absence of the clear cut triage process, which was adopted later by casualty clearing stations, often placed medical officers working in forward dressing stations such as Vailly with difficult professional dilemmas:

> A soldier was taken into Dr. Lancry's house suffering from a horrible wound of the abdomen. A piece of his abdominal wall about a s big as a pudding plate had been shot clean away, and one could see two or three broken ribs, a large piece of his liver, large intestine, small intestine, and omentum in the cavity. Although men have recovered many times in this war from wounds which apparently must have been fatal, in this case it was indisputable that recovery was totally out of the question. I advised that the man should be given a poisonous dose of morphia at once; I was overruled, and the man lingered on for two or three days occupying a bed which had better have been given to somebody less seriously wounded.

Over the course of the short period that Robinson had been at Vailly, nearly 500 wounded officers and men were successfully evacuated: eleven officers and 238 other ranks on the night of 15 September and another six officers and 241 other ranks the night after.

Chapter Five

THE 2ND DIVISION

AT PONT-ARCY on 13 September, 11/Field Company began work on the road bridge that had only been partly destroyed, while a mile and a half upstream the sappers of 5/Field Company started construction of a pontoon bridge, which was in use by 5pm that afternoon. One of the first battalions to cross the river at Pont-Arcy was the 2/Connaught Rangers who, under fire, used the single girder that remained of the original bridge and took up positions on the north bank where they remained covering the crossing by the remainder of 5 Brigade over the pontoon bridge.

The battalion, under the command of Major William Sarsfield, was ordered into Soupir to take up positions on the northern and western outskirts of the village. Further downstream, opposite Chavonne, 4 (Guards) Brigade, under the temporary command of Lieutenant

The destroyed bridge at Pont-Arcy and in the foreground the pontoon bridge used by the 2nd Division on 14 September.

A completely devastated Chavonne in 1917. Note the two French soldiers bottom right.

Colonel Fielding, was assembled to begin crossing the canal at Cys-la-Commune. They had arrived late and it was not until noon that they were ready to cross. Notwithstanding the information that Chavonne was apparently only lightly held, the approaches to the village were distinctly hazardous for the infantryman. The 800 yards wide stretch of ground between the canal bridge at Cys and the river crossing at Chavonne was devoid of all cover and offered no protection to assaulting infantry. On the northern bank the partially wooded ground rose steeply from the river, providing cover for a concealed enemy who had the benefit of excellent fields of fire over the whole area. If the village and the commanding heights above it were held in force and the rearguard determined to resist, a successful crossing would be very much in the balance.

With the three remaining battalions of the brigade in support, it fell to the 2nd Battalion Coldstream Guards (2/Coldstream) to test the strength and resolve of the German rearguard. Captain Gilbert Follett and Number 2 Company soon came under heavy rifle and machine gun fire as they approached the canal bridge, prompting Lieutenant Colonel Pereira to send up two further companies to return fire from the canal bank.

By 4pm the Coldstream were on the river bank, where a leaking boat found by Lance Corporal Albert Milward provided the transport for Number 3 Company to begin establishing themselves on the northern bank. The Coldstream war diary records the 'considerable opposition from hostile infantry and machine guns and at least a squadron of German cavalry', which was met by the Coldstream's Number 3 Company as they fought their way up onto the heights of Les Crinons above the village. Meanwhile the Grenadiers had begun crossing the river a mile or so east of Chavonne using what the

74

regimental historian describes as, 'three or four boats of doubtful buoyancy'. Darkness and heavy rain overtook the crossing and Colonel Fielding was ordered to withdraw the brigade – except the Coldstream Company established at Les Crinons – to the safety of St Mard and Cys for the night.

14 September

At 1am Major Sarsfield took the decision to move the 2/Connaughts up to La Cour de Soupir Farm, which lay at the head of the valley through which the advance would take place. The Connaughts arrived at 5.30am and found no sign of the enemy. They were less than two miles from the Chemin des Dames ridge. The Guards Brigade was on the move by 4.50am and after a march of two miles 'in the pouring wet' they were over the pontoon bridge by 8.30am. Here a disgruntled Major Bernard Gordon Lennox felt he 'had to wait a long time before getting across as various artillery and other units had to get across [before us]'. The 2/Grenadiers were the leading battalion and moved off towards Soupir, leaving the remainder of the brigade to cross behind them. Major Gordon Lennox's diary:

Major Lord Bernard Gordon Lennox, 2/Grenadier Guards.

> *In Soupir we turned to our left, and, after about a mile or so, turned up the hill. It was not known whether these wooded heights were held or not – it was our job to find out – we soon did. No. 1 and ? of No. 2 [Company] formed the vanguard, and on barely reaching the top the advance party was fired on: we pushed on and two more platoons of No.2 were sent forward. Being second in command I had to stay behind. Pretty steady firing was now going on, and we – the main body – got heavily shelled as we came up the road, the Dutchmen [sic] apparently having the range to a nicety. At the top of the hill was the farm of La Cour de Soupir – a building we were to become intimately acquainted with during the next few days – held, or rather occupied, by a regiment, which shall be nameless.*

The 'nameless' regiment was of course the 2/Connaught Rangers who had occupied the farm and pushed out their outposts onto the high ground around Point 197 at La Croix sans Tête. At the time of the Connaughts arrival at the farm there had been no sign of any Germans in the vicinity. The Connaughts' war diary recounts the arrival of the Grenadier Guards, four hours later:

*At about 9.30am a small party of the Guards Brigade under an
officer forming the point of their advance guard arrived at the
farm, but no more of the brigade arrived until about 11.30am. At
about 10am a message despatched at 9.25am by motorcyclist was
received from HQ 5 Brigade, to whom the movements of the
Battalion had been reported, stating that it would be some time
yet before the Guards Brigade could arrive and instructing the
OC CRs not to leave his position until they were up and had
securely occupied the high ground about La Croix sans Tête. The
Battalion was ordered to close on Moussy as soon as that
position was secure.*

The Grenadier officer noted in the Connaught war diary was probably
19-year-old Second Lieutenant John Pickersgill-Cuncliffe; with him
was Major Gilbert Hamilton commanding No 1 Company and Captain
Cholmeley Symes-Thompson with half of No 2 Company, who had
been sent out as flank guard on the left. Whether all the Grenadiers
remained at the farm or continued uphill is unclear, but Cuncliffe and
his platoon certainly were ahead of the main body when the attack
began.

Nor do we know for sure if it was his warning, or that of the
Connaught outposts that Major Sarsfield received at about 10.30am,

La Cour de Soupir Farm before the war.

alerting him to a large body of German infantry approaching the farm. Sarsfield's response was immediate and the Connaughts were deployed east and west of the farm:

> The attack was supported by artillery fire and pushed forward with great vigour. The enemy endeavoured to turn our right flank by moving through the woods and, against our centre and left, he advanced across the open ground in very large numbers. By 10.30am approximately, in spite of his losses which were very heavy, he had almost succeeded in turning our right flank and, most of our men who were holding the position close to the farm on the west having been killed and wounded, the enemy had succeeded in pushing forward to within 100 yards of the farm.

As the German infantry advanced towards the farm, the Connaught outposts around Point 197 were driven in along with Lieutenant Cuncliffe and his men. During the initial clash with the leading elements of the enemy the young officer was wounded along with several of his men who were taken prisoner, although it appears Cuncliffe was left lying on the battlefield.

At the farm the situation was beginning to get desperate on the right flank in the wooded slopes of the Bois de la Bovette. In response Major George 'Ma' Jeffreys, who was in temporary command of the Grenadiers, sent three platoons of No 4 Company up to support Hamilton while Lieutenant Colonel Fielding sent the 3rd

The German view of Cour de Soupir Farm, taken from the direction of Ostel.

Battalion Coldstream Guards up to the farm, supported on the right by the whole of the Irish Guards under Major Herbert Stepney. The first indication that Major Jeffreys had of the Coldstream Guards moving up to the farm was when they passed the Grenadiers' headquarters. Jeffreys then met Lieutenant Arthur Smith, the Coldstream Adjutant:

> [He] told me that Major Matheson, their commanding officer, was moving up to Cour de Soupir. I went and met Matheson on the road by the farm. One company of the 3rd Battalion Coldstream had come into action west and north-west of the farm

and with our No 2 had driven back the Germans, who withdrew
some hundreds of yards on this side.

It was during a later conversation with Matheson that Jeffreys was told of the death of John Cuncliffe, who had been shot dead by a German officer as he lay wounded on the ground. The incident was verified by men of his platoon who had been taken prisoner when the Germans advanced and then subsequently abandoned when the situation was reversed. Jeffreys in his diary account tells us this officer was immediately shot by the advancing Coldstream.

Major George Darell Jeffreys, 2/Grenadier Guards.

But the battle was not yet over. Pressure now came onto the left flank and German infantry were only held off by Numbers 1 and 2 Companies of the 2nd Battalion Coldstream, who had been sent in support. The 2/Coldstream were until this point being held in brigade reserve and it was not long before their companies were sent to bolster the right flank defences, leaving a mere two platoons in reserve. The fighting in the wooded area on the right flank was rendered more difficult by the steep edge of the spur, which fell away sharply into the Braye valley below.

Although this action cleared the ridge to the right of the firing line, there was no further appreciable advance made here; but at least contact was made with Major Edward Armitage and the men of A and D Companies of the KRRC, who were working up the western edge of the Braye valley as part of 6 Brigade's advance.

Artillery support from XXXVI Brigade was not assisted by the early morning mist, whilst the dense woods up to and over the horizon lines severely hampered observation by artillery batteries in the valley bottom. The brigade's guns were in place north and east of Soupir and, as the mist cleared, the German observers on the height above were able to direct fire onto any movement – particularly onto the British batteries. However, the appearance of a section of 18-pounder guns from 71/Battery during the late afternoon did much to improve the situation on the right and assisted in repelling a counter attack just before dusk. Noticeably these guns were practically the only artillery support 4 Brigade had all day.

At noon, encouraged by their success in holding off the enemy, Matheson and Jeffreys felt the time had arrived to take the offensive.

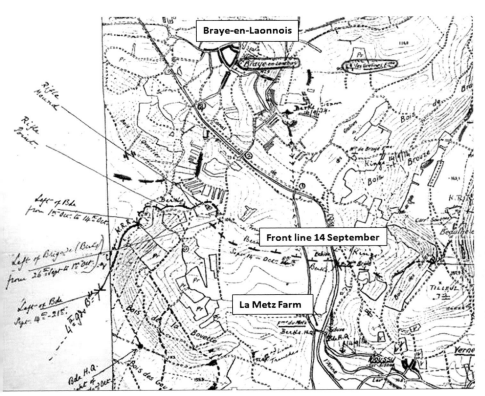

Map 9. British positions in the Braye valley on 14 September.

The German line was static in the turnip fields north of the farm and a spirited charge might just dislodge the enemy. But even before the Guardsmen had time to fix their bayonets and move forward, the Germans in the front line stood up and, with white flags waving, began to run forward with their hands up in surrender. George Jeffreys witnessed the event:

> *Unfortunately men of all units – Grenadiers, Coldstream, Connaught Rangers and Irish Guards – rushed forward to seize prisoners, and though both Matheson and I shouted to them to stand fast, we could not stop them and a confused mass of British and German soldiers was the result. On this mass the German soldiers in the rear at once opened fire, causing a number of casualties.*

Bernard Gordon Lennox watched aghast as both German and British soldiers fell, 'it was here most of the casualties occurred. The men learnt a lesson and there will not be much more notice taken of the white flag'. Jeffreys was sure there was never any premeditated treachery intended by the Germans, the leading line, he felt, had had enough and was very low in ammunition; the support line behind them, however, had no intention of surrendering and opened fire when the British troops ran forward.

The confusion that followed was the prelude to another attack, this time from the direction of Ostel. It was met with the customary Guards' resolve in the form of the 3/Coldstream machine gun section and the Grenadiers who lined the road north of the farm. The enemy attack soon died away but any thoughts of a further advance that afternoon seemed to be out of the question. The muddle that surrounded the fighting on 4 Brigade front was exacerbated by the news that the 3rd Division was in trouble at Vailly. Initial reports reaching I Corps Head Quarters at noon of a general retirement of 3rd Division units was fortunately corrected and by 2pm a more realistic appraisal of the situation was in front of Sir Douglas Haig. Realizing his left flank was under threat if the 3rd Division was pushed back to the river, he took steps to fill the gap between Chavonne and Vailly with 1 and 2 Cavalry Brigades, who were ordered to Soupir. Haig's own assessment of the situation is contained in I Corps war diary:

> A little later, an officer of the 15th Hussars rode in and reported that he had seen signs of our 3rd Division having been beaten back. The situation was critical. An advance by the enemy through Chavonne on Soupir would have cut the communications of the Corps; the last battalion of my reserve brigade had been drawn into the fight near Chivy, and I had no infantry which I could detach. The only men immediately at hand were a troop of the 15 Hussars and a squadron of the South Irish Horse. These I despatched at once to the threatened flank, and I also called upon the 2nd Cavalry Brigade to move to Soupir.

Captain Arthur Osburn, the medical officer with the 4/Dragoon Guards, remembered thinking that had the Germans counter attacked that afternoon things would have become very nasty. At about 4pm the brigade was halted in the woods to the north west of Soupir:

> Our General and some of his staff suddenly appeared. He evidently thought the situation, especially the position of the infantry who had crossed over behind us, precarious. He made us a speech ... "You must stay here at all costs! Everything may depend on you! Don't give an inch of ground. You may have to sustain seventy or eighty per cent casualties! Remain and die like gentlemen!" We looked at each other. Like Gentlemen – how else do people usually die?

Brigadier General de Lisle's speech certainly put 'the wind up' Osburn, who then 'made quite elaborate and feverish' medical arrangements for what he expected to be an 'enormous battle'.

The men of 1 Cavalry Brigade had evidently received a similar pep talk from Brigadier General Charles Briggs, as the 11/Hussars war diary betrays the urgency in which the regiment was ordered to Soupir:

Brigadier General Beauvoir de Lisle, commanding 2 Cavalry Brigade.
'Remain and die like gentlemen!'

> *We received an order to go to the left of the 1st Army [sic], Sir Douglas Haig is anxious about his left. The 2nd Army [sic] are not joined up with the first, and their right is being driven back over the river. We arrive at Soupir and take up a dismounted position on the left of our infantry [2/Ox and Bucks], also succeed in getting in touch with the right of the 2nd Army. The gap is a biggish one and a nasty bit of country. As we arrive, we see streams of wounded being brought down the track, the Guards have been having a bad time of it.*

The remainder of 1 Cavalry Brigade were deployed in a second line at Chavonne, which enabled the 11/Hussars to be withdrawn. Shortly afterwards the 2/Ox and Bucks were moved to Soupir, at which point Arthur Osburn felt it was almost an anticlimax that no German counter attack actually took place. The Dragoon Guards retired to Soupir Château with the Hussars.

Back at Cour de Soupir the day was drawing in but the German batteries continued to shell the British positions as they had for most of the day. Two companies of 2/Coldstream were sent down to Chavonne, where they spent a wet night with the cavalry; whilst the other and a further two were pushed across to the right where the Irish Guards were digging in. Artillery support we know, was practically non-existent – apart from the 71/Battery appearance at Cour de Soupir. XLI Brigade crossed at Bourg and then retired to Veil-Arcy, firing only twelve rounds all day – although 16/Battery was adamant that they 'stayed in action all day and night', but later conceding that they only 'blazed off a bit'. At least 35/Heavy Battery managed to fire thirty-four rounds, which was considerably more than 44/(Howitzer) Battery managed at Verneuil.

The Connaught Rangers were ordered back to Soupir as soon as it was dark. It has to be said that Major Sarsfield's early occupation of the farm on 14 September was carried out with the same spirit of initiative that drove Hunter-Weston's advance with 11 Brigade at Vénizel, but sadly it had the same outcome. What is difficult to understand is that at 5.30am the Connaughts were already halfway to the brigade objective, yet the first of the Guards battalions did not cross the river until 8.30am, despite the evidence from the Connaught's war diary – and that of 5 Brigade – both of which confirm that brigade headquarters were aware of the Connaughts' position at Cour de Soupir Farm.

Casualties

The 14 September had been a costly day for the 2nd Division. Three of the Connaughts' officers were killed with a further five wounded. In the ranks eighteen men were killed, 102 wounded and ninety-seven declared missing. The Grenadier losses were comparable: two officers killed, John Cuncliffe and Frederick des Voeux and six others wounded, in addition to seventeen other ranks killed, sixty-seven wounded and seventy-seven missing. The Coldstream casualties amounted to two killed – including Second Lieutenant Richard Lockwood – and sixty three wounded in the 2nd Battalion and twenty five killed and 153 wounded in the 3rd Battalion. The dead included the 26-year-old Lieutenant Percy 'Perf' Lyulph Wyndham, who had inherited the magnificent Clouds estate at East Knoyle two years previously on the death of his father, the Rt Hon George Wyndham MP. Perf had been married for less than two years to the Hon Diana Lister and was a cousin of the 17-year-old Edward 'Bim' Tennant, who himself would be killed serving with the Grenadier Guards in 1916.

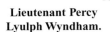

Lieutenant Percy Lyulph Wyndham.

After dark Matheson and Jeffreys reorganized their respective battalions from the 'proper mix-up' that the day's fighting had produced. It was agreed between the two battalion commanders that the Grenadiers would hold a line from the wood east of the farm as far as the Chavonne road, the 3/Coldstream along the Chavonne road to link up with the 2/Coldstream at Chavonne. On the right of the Grenadiers the Irish Guards were in contact with the 1/KRRC of 6 Brigade. Darkness was also the opportunity for recovering the wounded, some of whom had been lying out in front of the lines since the engagement began. Jeffreys had seen a 'considerable number' of both British and German as well as 'a very large number of dead Germans' as well as some who had been lying doggo and waited for darkness to give themselves up.

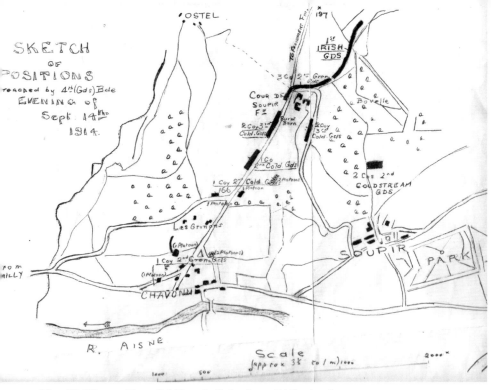

Map 10. The position of 4 Guards Brigade on 14 September.

The sheer numbers of wounded men threatened to overwhelm the battalion medical teams, who had been working feverishly for most of the day. The farmhouse was already full and the wounded now overflowed into the farm enclosure buildings but, even though as many of these men were got away that night by the few horse drawn ambulance wagons as could be spared, many of them were not taken down to Soupir until 16 September. Inevitably there were many wounded men in the Bois de la Bovette on the right flank who were not found and who died as a result.

6 Brigade

Despite being at Pont-Arcy on time, the four battalions of 6 Brigade did not complete their crossing until 8am, the narrow pontoon bridge put across by 5/Field Company only just able to cope with the number of troops and artillery batteries. The 1st Battalion Royal Berkshire Regiment (1/Berks) was clear of the bridge by 5am and advancing up the valley towards Braye-en-Laonnois, with two companies of the 1st Battalion King's Royal Rifle Corps, (1/KRRC) on each flank. The Braye valley also hosts the l'Oise à l'Aisne canal. This waterway –

83

running north-south through the centre of the 6 Brigade advance – cuts into the main ridge of the Chemin des Dames just south of Braye and effectively bisects the valley.

Lieutenant Alan Hanbury-Sparrow had a clear picture of the ground as he advanced with the Berkshires towards La Metz Farm:

Immediately on our west hand lies the Oise-Aisne canal, crossed by a small bridge at the large Ferme de Metz, and this is to be our right boundary. Beyond it is the country road running north and south, along which a few refugees are hastening. After a cannonade of some duration we move down towards this bridge, and see for the first time shells exploding in enormous clouds of black smoke – eleven inch, as we afterwards learn. As we approach, a young woman dragging a child by each hand rushes out of the farm and with terrified countenance scurries down the road.

At around 9am the forward company of the Berkshires had reached a line running east west of Le Moulin Brulé – about halfway between Moussy and Braye – when their advance was checked by heavy shell and rifle fire from both the Chemin des Dames ridge and the wooded areas on the sides of the valley.

The delay in responding to the enemy fire suggest the brigade had been, to some extent, taken aback by the intensity of the enemy fire and while the 1st Battalion King's Liverpool Regiment (1/King's) was brought forward on the Berkshires' right, the XXXIV Brigade guns were hurriedly brought into action on the southern slopes of the Moussy spur. Thus reinforced, 6 Brigade attack was launched at

The ruins of La Metz Farm, used by the 1/Berkshire Regiment as a battalion HQ.

10.30am, with the 1/King's on the east side of the canal and the Berkshires on the western side, flanked by the KRRC on the edges of the two spurs bordering the valley.

The attack was badly organized and seemingly hurriedly launched before the troops on the Moussy spur had time to get into position; the Berkshires advance up the valley soon outstripped the King's who in turn found themselves ahead of the KRRC flank companies. The sector given to the King's was from the canal to the top of the Moussy spur.

Lieutenant William Synge in B Company remembered that the attack was 'arranged on the map' and the 'factor of time prevented a systematic reconnaissance of the position'. The wooded nature of the ground and the haste in which the attack was planned was a recipe for confusion. The battalion war diary describes the King's advance taking place on both sides of the road from Moussy to the canal towards what Captain Hudson, the battalion Adjutant, describes as the Marval Ridge. This places them on the eastern side of the canal and approaching the ridge above les Grelines Farm that leads directly onto the Chemin des Dames. In his account Hudson acknowledges that the Berkshires got in front of them and describes how the King's worked along the edge of the Beauline Spur to the point where they came under fire from behind. Lieutenant Synge was unsure as to who was firing at them, 'someone said that it was our own people who were firing down on us from the hill top. Whether this was so I do not know, and probably never will know.' Whoever it was – friend or foe – the King's were now under fire from the German infantry to their front and also from the rear. Synge tells us his company then withdrew but at some during the advance an attempt was made to take the trenches on the ridge ahead of them, this time with the support of a platoon of 2/Worcesters. The attack was unsuccessful:

> It was impossible to get on until the high ground on our right had been cleared and Major S. then pulled the whole of the companies back. As the fire from behind made it nearly impossible to get forward ... Capt. Tanner and Ferneran were wounded. We took five Germans prisoners. Our losses were two officers killed and ninety [other ranks] killed and wounded.

However, the Berkshires, after crossing the canal just south of Braye, did get a footing on the small spur that runs down from the Chemin des Dames east of the village and by noon had two companies engaging a well dug in *28th Reserve Infantry Regiment* established on the steep slopes rising to the Chemin des Dames road. Hanbury-Sparrow recalled the moment he received orders to retire, orders, he noted with some anger, which his men did not hesitate to obey with some alacrity!

Major General Charles Monro, commanding the 2nd Division.

The 5 Brigade Advance

Even as 6 Brigade fell back in the face of a well dug in enemy, Douglas Haig, in consultation with the GOC 2nd Division, Major General Charles Monro, was planning a late-in-the-day push up the Beaulne spur in the hope of gaining the ridge before nightfall. The I Corps diarist described the advance: *The forward movement began about sunset, and the men, of whom many had been fighting hard since before daybreak, answered readily to my demand. They were met everywhere by very heavy rifle and gunfire ... Only in the centre, the 5th Brigade, moving along the eastern slopes of the Beaulne ridges, was able to get forward and continue its advance until it reached the ridge about Tilleul de Courtcon. In the dark General Haking failed to get in touch with the 1st Division, but his patrols found German outposts on both flanks. He consequently drew back his troops under cover of darkness to the neighbourhood of Verneuil.*

Haig's account does not refer to the confusion that must have existed that night on the Chemin des Dames ridge as isolated groups of infantry blundered around in the darkness. From Lieutenant Charles Paterson's account we know B and C Companies of the South Wales Borderers reached the ridge but, after being fired upon by outposts, retired after losing the two remaining companies in the dark! Lieutenant Colonel Northey and half the 1/KRRC reported reaching the Chemin des Dames at Tilleul de Courtcon, from where they moved west to Malval farm where, instead of finding British troops, 'they tumbled into a mass of Germans collecting near a large signal lamp'. The war diary gives no further information except to say they withdrew at midnight to Verneuil. The 2nd Battalion Highland Light Infantry (2/HLI) were also on the Chemin des Dames ridge at 12 midnight, whilst quite where and at what time the Worcesters gained the ridge is clouded by their war diary account, which reported their retirement at about 9pm after taking a few German prisoners.

It was during the early part of this advance that a Highland Light Infantry reservist, Private George Wilson, single handedly captured a German machine gun, turning it on the enemy before

Private George Wilson VC.

An artist's impression of Wilson capturing the German Machine gun before turning it on the enemy.

returning to his company with both the weapon and its ammunition. His award of the Victoria Cross took the total number of VCs won by the infantry on 14 September to three.

The attacks continue

Although the Guards had effectively stabilized the British line around Cour de Soupir Farm, the infantry attacks gradually gave way to a fairly regular recipe of shell fire. During a bombardment on 16 September, one 8-inch shell narrowly missed the farm buildings and landed in a nearby quarry where it exploded, killing and wounding over a hundred men of the Guards and Ox and Bucks Light Infantry. Major Bernard Gordon Lennox was in the quarry at the time, standing with Major Jeffreys and Captain Eben Pike:

> *In addition this same shell killed three officers of the Oxfords, and a medical officer. How it missed Jeffreys, George Powell, Eben Pike and self will forever remain a mystery. It killed and wounded people who were more under cover than we were, sitting all together. It killed and wounded people to our rear, front and left, but for some unknown reason we all escaped untouched.'*

Lieutenant James Huggan's death in the quarry was one of many that befell RAMC doctors attached to infantry battalions. The 25-year-old was a well known Scottish international rugby player and was killed the

87

day after another Scottish international, Lieutenant Ronald Simson, was killed in action serving with 16/Battery RFA.

Verneuil Château used by 5 and 6/Field Ambulance as an advanced dressing station.

Verneuil Château

The medical arrangements for the 2nd Division were initially overwhelmed with the sheer numbers of wounded. Two advanced dressing stations were established at Moussy and in some caves near Chivy, with the main dressing stations at the château at Verneuil and the rather ostentatious château at Soupir. At Verneuil conditions were made more difficult by the nearby artillery batteries that ensured the building was frequently shelled as German batteries searched for the British guns. 5/Field Ambulance took over the château at Verneuil around lunch time on 14 September; by the end of the day the building itself and the surrounding stables and outbuildings were filled with wounded, Major Frederick Brereton estimates some nine officers, 166 other ranks and fifty four Germans were admitted during the day, a number which included 48-year-old Lieutenant Colonel Charles Dalton, the 2nd Division ADMS. Dalton was severely wounded by a shell splinter as he was assisting with the carrying of casualties into the château. 6/Field

Ambulance arrived on the night of 14 September to assist in bringing in the wounded and over the course of the next twenty-four hours another seven officers and eighty five other ranks were admitted. But Verneuil had become too much of a shell trap to continue in its role as a divisional collecting station; it was becoming very exposed and three days later it received a direct hit, prompting the move to Viel-Arcy on 20 September.

Soupir Château

The château at Soupir did not take on the role of a main dressing station until 17 September, when 4/Field Ambulance moved into the building. Prior to that, 3/Cavalry Field Ambulance had occupied it, along with 1 and 2 Cavalry Brigades who, readers will recall, had been sent to reinforce the left flank after the 3rd Division got into difficulties. 3/Cavalry Field Ambulance had already been severely mauled by shellfire on the night of 15 September when a large shell fell amongst a group of horses and men at the château; five men were killed and a further eight were wounded.

The bombardment continued, forcing the ambulance to move south of the river but even as they crossed the river they attracted further salvoes, which followed them across the flat, open ground all the way to Viel-Arcy.

Soupir Château before the war.

The château building and its grounds were situated close to the church at Soupir. A construction of pretentious proportions, its grand architectural design even encompassed the stable block, a magnificent building and so ornate it was sometimes mistaken for the main building. Surrounded by elaborately manicured gardens and boasting a large lake to the southwest, the château was the home of Maria Boursin, the alleged mistress of the editor of the Paris newspaper *Le Figaro*, Gaston Calmette.

All this was to change on 17 September. Within days the three story building was catering for the seemingly continual stream of wounded who were being brought in from the surrounding area. Under the command of Major Percy Falkner, the château was taking in an average of fifty casualties per day on top of the German casualties being treated in the nearby church. Soupir Château remained in the hands of 4/Field Ambulance until they finally left on 12 October, by which time the building had suffered hugely from German artillery and the ravages of war. Maria Boursin also owned property in Paris to which she hastily retired when war reached the Aisne. By 1918 – after three battles on the Aisne had run their course – the building was completely destroyed and Maria Boursin never returned to Soupir to rebuild her home.

Chapter Six

THE 1ST DIVISION

AT BOURG-ET-COMIN there were two canal bridges – one of which was an aqueduct – and a road bridge that crossed the river. An initial cavalry reconnaissance reported the village clear of enemy troops but when Lieutenant Robert Featherstonehaugh and a troop of B Squadron, 4/Dragoon Guards, arrived they were met with a hail of gunfire from entrenched enemy infantry along the canal bank. Similarly, when A

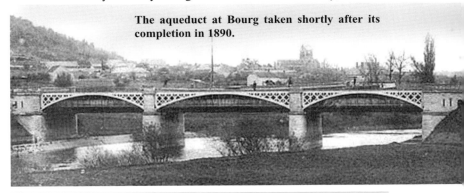

The aqueduct at Bourg taken shortly after its completion in 1890.

The aqueduct was completely destroyed during the war.

The aqueduct today.

Squadron approached the bridges at Villiers – which had both been destroyed – the canal bank was found to be occupied by an enemy rearguard.

Fortunately the two canal bridges at Bourg were intact and taken by the dragoons under heavy fire. Given the task confronting them, casualties were extraordinarily light: only one officer and three men killed. When 28-year-old Captain Gerald 'Pat' Fitzgerald, the machine gun officer, went down with a bullet between the eyes, Arthur Osburn was only yards away. 'Fitzgerald was unconscious when I got to him, his wound no bigger than a blue pencil mark in the centre of his forehead. Then in a moment he was gone.'

Once across the canal it became apparent that, although the road bridge had been destroyed, the aqueduct carrying the canal over the river was intact. Apart from an 'uncomfortable quarter of an hour', when the cavalrymen were caught in crossfire, Osburn recorded his relief in watching the defending German rearguard being the subject of some accurate shellfire and eventually retreating towards the wooded slopes of the high ground to the north.

The crossing of several thousand infantrymen and innumerable wheeled transports over the aqueduct made life quite difficult for the sappers of 23/Field Company. Charged with maintaining the integrity of the towpath, Lieutenant Richard Bond was relieved to find the canal towpath was wide enough but also realized it was not possible to leave the path for another mile – until the Bourg-Vailly road crossed the canal – and began supervising the construction of a corduroy road to enable the traffic to leave the towpath:

> The towpath was hard put to it to stand the strain of the traffic, and the Company was fully employed in keeping the surface in condition, rapidly filling up holes with whatever material was handy, in intervals, between units, and suffering the objurgations of gunners temporarily held up by more than usually extensive repairs, whilst from time to time a long-distance shrapnel shell from the Chemin des Dames would fall with a sizzle into the water.

With the cavalry across the river, the waiting infantry and artillery units who were gathering south of the Canal Latéral began moving to join them. Lieutenant Evelyn Needham had been on the road since 4am with his company of 1st Battalion Northamptonshire Regiment (1/Northamptons) and arrived south of Bourg to find the 'cavalry and artillery hotly engaged with the enemy on the far side of the river'. Glad of the rest, they were held up for three or four hours before the order to advance saw the battalion crossing the aqueduct. 'Oddly enough', wrote Needham, 'I have no recollection of this crossing beyond the fact that we doubled across as fast as we could, so as to get under cover on the far side.'

Brigadier General Ivor Maxse's 1 (Guards) Brigade and Herman Landon's 3 Infantry Brigade followed on and advanced northeast towards Paissy, where they took up a position to the left of 2 Cavalry Brigade. At 4pm Edward Bulfin's 2 Brigade was across the river and gathered west of Paissy in and around Moulins, releasing 2 Cavalry Brigade, who withdrew to Bourg. By 6pm on 13 September the last man of the 1st Division was on the north bank of the Aisne.

That night the 1st Division and 2 Cavalry Brigade occupied a line Paissy-Moulins-Oeuilly-Bourg, so Brigg's 1 Cavalry Brigade was sent back across the river and all in all the prospects for the next day looked good. Haig was still working on intelligence that suggested the enemy in front of him was thinly deployed; he had little, if any, idea of the movement of the German *VII Reserve Corps* that had already arrived on the Chemin des Dames.

The local movement of German rearguards appeared to suggest the German army was still in retreat, a belief that was repeated in the GHQ Operational Order No 24 issued at 6pm on 13 September with the

Map 11. The canal and river crossings at Bourg-et-Comin.

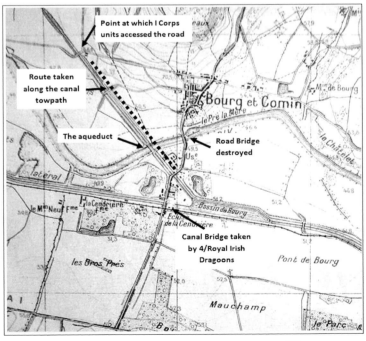

93

optimistic instruction to 'continue the pursuit to-morrow at 6am and act vigorously against the retreating enemy'.

2 Brigade

The plan for 2 Brigade's attack was simple enough: under the immediate command of Lieutenant Colonel Pearce-Serocold, both the 2/KRRC and the 2/Royal Sussex would move quickly to occupy the high ground above the hamlet of Troyon. Pearce-Serocold would move to take the crossroads at Cerny while Lieutenant Colonel Ernest Montresor remained in support with the 2/Royal Sussex at Vendresse until required.

The 1/Northamptons, under the command of Lieutenant Colonel Edward Osborne Smith, were under orders to climb the spur above Moulins and attack the ridge on the left of the 1st Battalion Queen's Royal West Surrey Regiment (1/Queen's) from 3 Brigade, who were detailed as flank guard on the extreme right. We will follow the fortunes of the Northamptons and the Queen's later.

The early start on 14 September was the beginning of a day that would be forever etched in the memory of Sergeant Bradlaugh Sanderson. Apart from the 2.30am start in heavy mist and rain that fell heavily on his already tired limbs, he recalled 'we had no overcoat, only a waterproof sheet'. He was now advancing with D Company of 2/KRRC and feeling the cold:

Lieutenant Colonel Ernest Montresor, commanding 2/Royal Sussex.

We moved out of Paissy at 2.30am past the outposts and crept silently up the hill with fixed bayonets. We were told that we were going to surprise an outpost on front, that's all ... We went gingerly through a village – Troyon – and up the slope of a big spur in front. We got to the top, reformed and were going through a cutting in the hillside nearly at the top, marching on either side of the road in single file. Suddenly a squad of cavalry came dashing through which was upsetting the whole show.

Whether the Germans were all asleep or not, Sanderson was of the opinion the cavalry's blunder into the German line proved their salvation, alerting the company to the German presence. The German line was positioned astride the sunken road at the point where a track that ran down from the Chemin des Dames cut across the road; the alerted picquet began firing wildly straight down the road, one round hitting Lieutenant Riversdale Grenfell, who was killed immediately.

D Company of the Rifles stood their ground, the company commander, Captain Augustus Cathcart, sent Lieutenant Seymour

Mellor back to report to Lieutenant Colonel Pearce-Serocold, who was with A Company sheltering under the lee of the hillside near Troyon. Cathcart's men were being fired on from three sides but refused to give ground; following his platoon commander, Second Lieutenant Stuart Davison, Sanderson heard Cathcart shouting 'extend over the ridge right and left!':

> *The day was just breaking when we got into position. We had two killed in a few seconds. Then the Germans turned two machine guns on to us from a haystack, not thirty yards to our front. My officer seized hold of a man's rifle, at the same time shouting "There are hundreds of Germans behind that haystack." Then he stood up and deliberately fired, standing. I shouted "Get down sir!". He was shot through the eye immediately and died a few minutes after. Before he did that however he said, "Hold onto this position as it is on the flank. Don't retire until you get orders".*

Out on the right flank, Sanderson and his company were soon reinforced by A Company at about 5.45am, which is more or less the time B Company appeared on the left flank. The battalion was now astride the sunken road, dawn had broken and fortunately the mist was still clinging to the hillside, masking the British positions a little from the German guns which were in position some 600 yards in front. But from the weight of fire being directed onto the KRRC it was obvious this was no rearguard but a substantial body of troops and reinforcements were needed urgently. Pearce-Serocold responded quickly and dispatched a runner to Lieutenant Colonel Montresor, requesting that the Royal Sussex reinforce the firing line.

The unmistakable noise of battle on the heights above had already alerted the Sussex and, sensing he would soon be needed, Montresor had already moved the battalion up from Vendresse in anticipation. By 6.30am they were deployed on the left and right of the KRRC.

The arrival of the Sussex lengthened the firing line and enabled A and B Companies of the Sussex to outflank the German position on the left; the Sussex war diary notes with some satisfaction that 'fire was opened and continued for some minutes when it was seen that a large number of Germans were putting up their hands to surrender'. Sanderson was one of the many witnesses to the events that followed. 'I heard a lot of shouting and everybody was standing up. The Germans had put up a white flag and were coming in by hundreds to surrender.' As the Sussex men rose to their feet to bring in the prisoners, the Germans in the trenches behind them opened fire on both their own men and the British. The deadly combination of their own riflemen and the rapid fire being returned by the British riflemen cut down many of the hapless German infantrymen in the act of surrendering; nevertheless, some 300 of the enemy were taken prisoner. It was a similar occurrence to that witnessed by Major Jeffreys at Cour de Soupir and was the prelude to a number of so-called 'white flag' incidents that enraged the British notion of 'fair play'.

Another similar incident involving the Sussex occurred a short time later on the right of the line when a German firing line was again outflanked and surrendered, On this occasion the surrendering Germans were fired on by two of the guns from the German battery that was near the Sucrerie. We are told that practically all these men were shot down by their own side. Whether Sanderson was confusing the two surrender episodes is unclear from his account but he does express his shock when the German gunners deliberately opened fire on their own. 'I had a sneaking fancy all wasn't right', he wrote, 'then they deliberately opened fire at short range.'

With two battalions now fully committed, Bulfin, realizing he needed to reinforce the firing line, ordered the 1st Battalion Loyal North Lancashire Regiment (1/Loyals) to move up the hill from Vendresse where they had been placed in reserve earlier in the morning. On their way up to Troyon they passed German prisoners being escorted down towards the river, Second Lieutenant James Hyndson, marching with B Company, noticed the enemy soldiers 'were in tears'. Hyndson was the officer commanding Number 8 Platoon:

On approaching the crest of hill we come on signs of conflict. Helmets lying all over the place and also rifles. A good deal of blood, and several wounded and dead lying about. We reach the crest and halt just under it. The bullets now seem to be coming from all directions. After a short rest we are ordered to attack factory.

Bulfin's orders from division were not to push on beyond the Chemin des Dames, but as yet the strongpoint ahead of him – the Sucrerie and the adjoining farmhouse – was preventing his brigade from reaching their objective. This sector of the line was defended by three battalions of the German *27 Reserve Infantry Regiment* and the guns of *14 Reserve Field Artillery Regiment*, and it was against these men that the Loyals advanced. Facing the barrage of fire that was being directed at them, Hyndson described his platoon's advance:

I extend my platoon after Loomes (he is far in front of his platoon waving them on; this is the last I saw of him). Loomes is on my right and Goldie is on my left. Had only gone a hundred yards under a perfect hail of bullets when I heard a singing sound on my right. Two eight-inch shells had pitched 20 yards to my left and blew sky high a few of my platoon. The shells emitted a tall cloud of black dust and smoke. Truly terrible missiles. We go forward, but as yet I can see nothing. At last we reach the firing line. How anyone reached it is beyond comprehending. And such a line. All manner of regiments are there, and the dead and wounded are lying around in scores. We carry the factory and hold on like grim death. Allason is a little to my right, and Goldie landed up to me. He shortly afterwards moved off to the left by rolling on his side, and that was the last I saw of him.

The Loyals carried the attack to the factory building as ordered, with B and D Companies advancing across a quarter of a mile of open ground; their casualties – which were alarmingly heavy – included the commanding officer, Major Walter Lloyd and his adjutant, Captain Richard Howard-Vyse, who were reported to have been killed in the first rush.

But their advance provided the catalyst and, with the Loyals now in possession of the building, Lieutenant Vere Dashwood and his machine gun section from the Royal Sussex brought up their two Vickers guns to a point where they could bring a heavy fire onto the German batteries to the east. Dashwood's men effectively prevented any attempts by the German gunners to withdraw their guns; each time horses and limbers were brought up they were shot down by the fire from the Sucrerie building, 'the guns of both batteries became derelict' exclaimed the Sussex war diary. The Loyals' war diary suggests the factory building was occupied sometime after 11am but by 12.30pm they were running short of ammunition. Lieutenant Hyndson again:

The German machine guns were very nasty; they keep traversing up and down our line. A great increase in the noise of cracking whips overhead always heralded their return. Many men were hit and the casualties became truly appalling. We get no

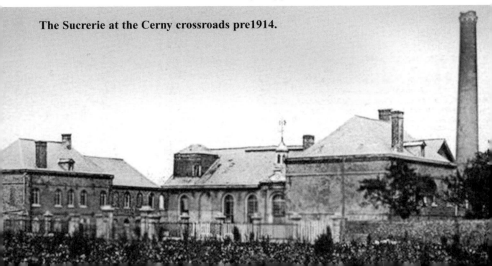

The Sucrerie at the Cerny crossroads pre1914.

Brigadier General Edward Bulfin. He commanded the 2 Infantry Brigade at Cerny.

reinforcements or ammunition and soon exhaust our supply. Germans heavily counter attack.

Sanderson had lost nearly half his men and was also running short of ammunition, sending word for more of both: 'I got the ammunition but no reinforcements'. The situation was becoming desperate, even more so since the German line was being strengthened by units of the German *X Corps* from the *Second Army* and a Horse Artillery *Abteilung* from the *9th Cavalry Division*.

1 Brigade

Leaving their bivouacs at Paissy, the 1/Coldstream was detailed as advance guard to the brigade moving at 6.45am through Moussy and Vendresse. Avoiding the sunken road – where the initial engagement had begun earlier that morning – the battalion climbed the wooded slopes above Vendresse in single file to reach the high ground of the Troyon spur in order to approach Cerny from the southwest. Extending across the flat top of the plateau and guided by the tall chimney of the Sucrerie, which they could just make out through the mist and driving rain, the battalion, led by Lieutenant Colonel John Ponsonby, soon came under heavy rifle and shell fire, Ponsonby noting with some pride that 'the men advanced splendidly, no man hesitated, although many were falling on all sides'.

Meanwhile the Cameron Highlanders and the 1/Black Watch discovered one of the numerous tracks that ran up onto the spur from the southwest and had already arrived on the top near the quarries on Mount Faucon. Extending into skirmishing lines, they moved between two of the quarries for some 500 yards and lay down with the Black Watch to their right.

Lieutenant Colonel John Ponsonby, circa 1897. Ponsonby commanded 1/ Coldstream Guards.

At 7.00am the advance began again, this time towards the distant shape of the factory chimney; but as soon as they left the cover of the wooded area they came under attack from the front and the right. While A Company took the brunt of this attack, the remaining companies continued, extending their lines with one company of the Black Watch on the right and the elements of the Scots Guards on the left. It must have been a magnificent sight and one that the Germans on the Chemin des Dames had cause to remember as the Highlanders swept through the enemy trenches and took up a firing line eighty yards beyond the road.

With two half companies across the road, the remainder of the Cameron Highlanders moved up the small Blanc Mont spur where they were able to bring fire to bear on the Chemin des Dames ridge. The battalion now occupied an S shaped firing line which at 8.00am was attacked along its whole length. The weight of enemy infantry eventually forced the right flank to fall back behind the bank of the Chivy road.

Attacks on the battalion continue throughout the morning, during which time Lieutenant Colonel McLachlan was wounded; while on the left of the line C Company were introduced to the white flag ruse:

No 11 Platoon of C Company on the left (2/Lt Smith-Sligo) had 13 men killed altogether owing to the fact a body of Germans advanced waving their rifles above their heads and apparently wishing to surrender. On the platoon going forward they were decimated by the fire of another German line behind, and the line apparently wishing to surrender lay down and probably fired also.

Although this 'white flag' incident may have been the same one as described by Sanderson, it is possible it was an entirely separate event, bearing in mind that the Camerons were west of the Sucrerie and the men of 11 Platoon went forward to receive the surrendering Germans. Nevertheless, it appears that this time it was a deliberate ploy by the Germans to lure the unsuspecting British infantry out of cover.

Lieutenant Colonel Ponsonby's advance into Cerny
In the intervening time – while the Camerons and Black Watch were dealing with the left flank – John Ponsonby and the 1/Coldstream reached the brick wall that surrounded the Sucrerie at about the time the factory chimney was brought down by enemy shellfire. Thus we can put a time of about 9.30am when Ponsonby with a mixed party of men from all regiments and Number 2 Company of the Coldstream pushed on over the road itself:

We made rushes by sections and got to the sunken road and pressed on forward to a village, Cerny by name. At this time I suppose we were about 100 to 150 strong, but under the circumstances it was impossible to estimate numbers, we could only hope the remainder of the battalion would come on ... Charlie Grant took 50 men down one side of the village, Aldam, Paget and myself keeping down the centre of the village with the remainder. In the village I found a large German ambulance corps; a German colonel came out of one of the houses. I saw he had about 20 medical officers with him and there appeared to be a whole medical arrangement and appliances in the house.

On the far side of the village they stumbled across German troops. At first Ponsonby thought they were British or even French troops but quickly realized they were in fact the enemy who, after a sharp shoot-out, vanished into the gloom. At the northern edge of the village the party were discovered and John Ponsonby was hit in the ankle. Surrounded, they remained in the wood until dark when they managed to evade the enemy during a rainstorm:

We passed German troops within 50 yards, but by keeping as quiet as possible and with the aid of the storm of wind and rain, we passed through them unobserved. We could only go at the rate of about one mile an hour, as I could not be carried any faster ... At 5am we got into a main road and walked in to one of our field ambulances at the village of Vendresse.

The Northamptons and Queen's on the Chemin des Dames

A mile further east along the ridge the Queen's, together with the 1/Northamptons, had also advanced over the road, meeting little opposition until the ground fell away from them by La Bovelle Farm. Here the two battalions found themselves looking down into the valley of the Ailette, which separated them from the German 8-inch artillery batteries on the far rim.

Nothing was done to capitalize on this advance but the Queen's did wreak considerable havoc with their machine guns on German troops who were unfortunate enough to be moving to the east. It is almost heartbreaking to ponder on the fact that at two separate points along the Chemin des Dames, barely a mile apart, the German line had been infiltrated with very little difficulty by a substantial number of British troops who were forced to withdraw in the absence of any support.

The Northamptons advance was graphically described by Lieutenant Needham, who advanced with the battalion up the Moulins spur and was in sight of the Chemin des Dames at 11.30am.

German heavy artillery being pulled into position on the Aisne.

Needham, known to his friends as 'Jack', could see the ridge to his front and had a grandstand view of the battle around the Sucrerie:

> It was still very wet and misty and we could only just make out the ridge opposite with its telegraph poles running along the Chemin des Dames, its haystacks and its factory chimney. But we could see the 1st and 2nd Brigades attacking the terraces to our left front, and a wonderful sight it was – just like watching a field day on the Fox Hills or Salisbury Plain, except there were continuous puffs of smoke about, both on the ground and in the air, and that one saw little figures collapse and lie still! The noise of gun fire, machine guns and rifles was incessant, but only an occasional spent bullet came over us on our hill, or a very occasional shrapnel burst. Why the Germans did not plaster our hill-top with shrapnel I cannot imagine.

Lieutenant Evelyn 'Jack' Needham. 1/Northamptonshire Regiment.

Ordered to advance in extended order, C and B Companies moved up to take a position on the left of the Queen's. Needham and his platoon were part of C Company and were initially masked from enemy observation by the mist and a shallow depression in the ground. Intent on maintaining pace and focused very much on staying alive, Needham did not notice passing over the first line of German trenches as they topped the rise and halted on the road itself. After straightening up their line with the Queen's they went on:

About 150 yards beyond the road the gradient begins to flatten out, and it was soon pretty evident that we had been seen! Everything seemed to open on us at once – rifles, machine guns, artillery, etc. The noise was deafening, the rifle and machine gun bullets made a noise like a stock whip being cracked in one's ear as they passed ... It never seemed to stop. Nothing seemed to stop. Men were falling now right and left. We were advancing in two lines, and my platoon was in the second line ... on we went – it seemed like miles that we had advanced, whereas it was only about three hundred yards. Men continued to fall, the noise continued deafening, but we could see no shells bursting over the enemy, and we were cursing them accordingly.

As their advance ground to a halt, Needham recalled lying flat on the ground for about twenty minutes 'being utterly unable to find out what was happening elsewhere'.

There were no orders and they lay there not knowing whether to advance, retire or maintain their positions. 'Then the rain stopped and the mist began to clear, and presently to our joy shrapnel started to burst about twenty to thirty yards in front of us, right over the German trenches.' The Northamptons were finally ordered to retire by Lieutenant Colonel Osborne-Smith, which they did under the cover of shrapnel fire from 114/Battery. The Queen's were also forced to pull back after the French Colonial Division had failed to make headway on their right, digging in along the line of the Chemin des Dames around 4.30pm with the Northamptons.

XXV Brigade RFA

The clearing mist had enabled Lieutenant Colonel John Geddes' XXV Brigade RFA finally to bring their guns into action. Up to this point in the battle the British brigades fighting along the Chemin des Dames had been without artillery support; bringing guns to bear on the enemy positions was impossible in the misty conditions, as without clear observation there was every possibility the gunners would be firing on British troops. Here the Germans had a clear advantage over the British gunners as their guns were in position well before the attack began and they knew the dispositions of their troops; but at least the mist provided some cover under which the gunners of 116/Battery could manhandle their guns up above Troyon.

They were now in action just behind the firing line. Although this single battery could hardly be called artillery support they did fire some 1200 rounds of ammunition – the battery was kept supplied with ammunition entirely by hand – and at least managed to redress the balance of firepower a little. The welcome shrapnel that Needham saw bursting over the German trenches was most likely from 114/Battery, which was firing from a field just east of Troyon, 'their fire caused the enemy's rifle and machine gun fire to lessen a bit, which was a real blessing'.

Retirement from the Sucerie
Although the clearing mist had enabled the British gunners to get to work, it also precipitated a series of renewed German attacks on the British positions, particularly on the Sucerie. At 1pm an attack launched at the entire frontage of 1 Guards Brigade and 2 Brigade pushed the British out of the buildings – which at the same time exposed the Camerons' right flank – forcing their eventual retirement back towards the Chivy valley. By this time it had also become obvious that the 2nd Division on the left had not made progress and their hoped for appearance on the Chemin des Dames was not going to happen. The orders to withdraw from the Sucerie were prompted by shell fire from

The hamlet of Troyon in ruins. Note the ridge of the Chemin des Dames on the skyline.

the German batteries on the far side of the Ailette valley. James Hyndson was told to get his men out by Captain Lionel Allason. There were not many left:

> *Allason orders me to retire and I do so with two Loyal North Lancs, three Black Watch, two Cameron Highlanders. We move back at a fast double and, coming to a Donga, take shelter there. We are subjected to a terrific bombardment and it is death to show a hand. The shells seem to come right in and sweep the hole out. We lie there for some time and then move a little further back. I strike the Gloucester Regiment ... they have come up to support us and have had no casualties. They are all very eager to go on.*

Sergeant Sanderson gave the order himself to what was left of his platoon:

> *I gave the order to retire, calling one after the other, those remaining to keep up a rapid fire so as to render the retirement effective. But the hounds got a Maxim onto us. The chap next to me got hit in the leg and arm and he said "Don't leave me Sergeant." Another chap and I got to him and dragged him along, crawling until we got him to a coal box hole. The fates were unkind for the other chap got hit so I left my water bottle and scooted ... I got back with four men out of sixteen.*

As 1 Brigade fell back from the factory, the Camerons and Black Watch fought a desperate fighting withdrawal until they reached the shelter of the woods north of Vendresse while smaller parties worked their way down the Chivy valley. But one party of some sixty Camerons, under the command of Major Hon Alfred Maitland, stubbornly hung onto the ground they had taken at Blanc Mont. Seriously short of ammunition, they resorted to collecting rounds from the dead and wounded before

they were forced to withdraw, leaving Maitland dead behind them.

Devotion to duty was clearly very much to the fore amongst the ranks of the Cameron Highlanders on that shrapnel torn ridge. During the fighting in the morning, when Lieutenant James Matheson was badly wounded, he was carried to a place of safety by Private Ross Tollerton who, after the battalion retired, returned to his platoon officer to take him down to the dressing station but found himself and the wounded Matheson cut off by advancing Germans.

For three days Ross Tollerton – wounded in the head, back and hand – remained with the stricken Matheson before he was able to carry him down to Chivy. His award of the Victoria Cross was well deserved.

Private Ross Tollerton VC.

German counter attack

As the fighting around Cerny ebbed and flowed, a German counter attack on the I Corps left flank was organized to divert some of the pressure away from the hard pressed German *27 Reserve Brigade*. Three battalions and two machine gun companies from *25 Reserve Brigade* launched their attack at 10am with the intention of driving a wedge between Haig's two divisions. This attack was met by the 1/Battalion South Wales Borderers and the 2/Welsh with assistance from 113 and 46/Batteries; and from all accounts the German attack appears to have been stopped very effectively by the two 3 Brigade battalions. It was during this engagement that Lance Corporal William Fuller of the 2/Welsh won the second Victoria Cross of the day for carrying a wounded officer, Captain Mark Haggard, a nephew of the novelist Henry Rider Haggard, to safety. Sadly, Haggard died from his wounds the next day.

Captain Mark Haggard.

Lance Corporal William Fuller VC.

Casualties

1st Division casualties from the fighting on 14 September alone amounted to over 3,500 officers and men and many of these were from the two highland regiments. The Cameron Highlanders alone lost some 600 officers and men and amongst the casualties suffered by the 1/Black Watch was their commanding officer, 44-year-old Adrian Grant-Duff, Major Lord Stewart Murray and Lieutenants Cumming, Don and Boyd. Six other Black Watch officers were wounded, along with forty other ranks killed, 112 wounded and thirty five missing. Lieutenant Hon Gerard Freeman-Thomas was the only officer killed in the 1/Coldstream but ten others, including John Ponsonby, were wounded, along with 343 other ranks, many of whom were posted as missing. Edward Bulfin reported forty one officers and 926 NCOs and men killed, wounded or missing from 2 Brigade; of these the Royal Sussex lost five officers killed, including the commanding officer, Ernest Montresor and four other officers

Lieutenant Colonel Adrian Grant-Duff, commanding officer of the 1/Black Watch.

George Hutson competing in the 5000 m at the Stockholm Olympic Games in 1912. Hutson is pictured in third place wearing the union flag on his vest.

wounded. Eleven other ranks were killed, seventy nine wounded and 114 were still missing by nightfall, many of whom were wounded and still lying out on the battlefield. Amongst the Sussex dead was 25-year-old Sergeant George Hutson of B Company. Hutson competed for Great Britain in the 1912 Stockholm Olympics, winning a bronze medal in the 5000 metres and a team bronze in the 3000 metre team race.

The Loyals suffered badly in their advance to the Sucrerie and reported seventy-eight other ranks and twelve officers killed, wounded or missing. Included amongst the dead was their commanding officer, Major Walter Lloyd, who was only in his third day of command after the death of Lieutenant Colonel Guy Knight at Priez on 11 September. There is no accurate figure for the number of men wounded or missing from the battalion but from the war diary we know casualties were 'very heavy indeed'. The officer casualties in the 2/KRRC were eight killed and missing – of whom only two were recovered for burial – and seven wounded, which together with the 306

Vendresse Château was used as a dressing station by 3/Field Ambulance.

other ranks killed, wounded or missing represented a sizeable proportion of the battalion.

Initially the wounded were brought down to dressing stations which had been established in the Mairie at Vendresse and at the crossroads south of Vendresse near La Mal Bâtie Farm. But these two aid points were completely overwhelmed early on in the morning by the sheer numbers of wounded men flooding down from the fighting on the Chemin des Dames.

Consequently Vendresse Château, belonging to the Comte de la Maisonneuve, was taken over by 3/Field Ambulance and, a little further south, at Moulins, 1/Field Ambulance established itself in a cluster of buildings that were sheltered from shellfire by the high ground above. 2/Field Ambulance originally set up its dressing station in a farm near Oeuilly but shell fire soon encouraged a rapid move south of the river to Villers, where they established themselves in the château and local Mairie. It was not long before the relatively secure Villers became the divisional collecting station. Crisis point was reached on 15 September when the numbers of wounded pouring into Villers were getting beyond the available resources of the field ambulance staff. An appeal to the French for assistance resulted in twenty motor ambulances and drivers arriving the next day to move wounded to Fère-en-Tardenois and Bazoches. This was the first instance in which British wounded had been transported by motor ambulance *en masse*.

Close to the firing line the advanced dressing stations – which in many cases were combined with regimental aid posts – were at Beaulne, Troyon, Chivy and Paissy.

15 September

In contrast to the fighting of the previous day, 15 September was relatively quiet. There were several intense periods of shelling by both sides, during which Bombardier Ernest Horlock of 113/Battery won the Victoria Cross during a local attack near Vendresse. His citation in the *London Gazette* of 25 November reads: 'For conspicuous gallantry on 15th September, near

Bombardier Ernest Horlock VC.

Vendresse, when his Battery was in action under a heavy shell fire, in that, although twice wounded, he persisted on each occasion in returning to lay his gun after his wound had been dressed'. Promoted to sergeant two days later, he was drowned when the troopship SS *Aragon* was sunk on 30 December 1917. On 24 May 2001 the parish of Langrish in Hampshire unveiled a memorial to Ernest Horlock in St John's Church. The event was attended by Horlock descendants from all over the world. A contingent from 10/(Assaye) Battery – the descendants of 113/Battery and the holders of Horlock's VC – was also present.

Chapter Seven

STALEMATE AND THE 6TH DIVISION

THE HEAVY BRITISH casualties sustained on 14 September can be regarded as the final tremor in the wave of optimism that had been expressed in GHQ Operational Order Number 24 on 13 September. The next day Douglas Haig and William Pulteney, commanding III Corps, were ordered to consolidate their positions but Smith-Dorrien was instructed to continue the attack with II Corps. In reality the two divisions of II Corps were in no position to maintain their attack on 15 September, particularly with the lack of effective artillery support that had been a feature of the previous day's offensive; in fact it was not until 19 September that any replacements for the 18-pounder artillery pieces lost at Le Cateau began to arrive.

Major General William Pulteney, commanding III Corps on the Aisne.

On 14 September the 3rd Division had only just managed to stem a German counter attack and Fergusson's 5th Division had made very little headway on the Chivres spur. The complete lack of progress by Fergusson's division on 15 September, together with the withering barrage of shellfire that descended on the whole BEF frontage, finally convinced a wavering Sir John French that the German retreat was over. Operational Order Number 26, issued by GHQ at 8.30pm on 15 September, effectively signalled the beginning of positional warfare on the Aisne.

A British 18-pounder artillery piece. This weapon was the mainstay of the Royal Field Artillery during the Great War.

On either flank of the BEF the French armies had reached similar conclusions.

German reinforcements had successfully seen off any ambition the French armies may have had of breaking through. On 14 September the French XVIII Corps, under General de Mas-Latrie, had lost Craonne and Craonnelle and to the west General Victor Boëlle's IV Corps had failed to turn the flank of von Kluck's *First Army* at Nampcel. While deadlock looked almost certain it was vital to hold the Germans on the Aisne if the possibility of turning their flank west of the Oise was to become reality. As you would expect, such a move had not by-passed German thinking at OHL. Eric von Falkenhayn, who had succeeded von Moltke on 15 September as Chief of the German General Staff, was only too aware that the German right flank was 'in the air' and without any appreciable reserves behind it. With a strategy that to an extent mirrored that of the French and British, he ordered a series of strong counter attacks along the Aisne front to the west and east of Reims in order to hold the allied armies so as to allow German units to be moved to the west. These attacks fell largely on the British sector.

The 6th Division
Although the 6th Infantry Division was mobilized on 4 August 1914, it remained in the Cambridge area until 7 September before finally embarking for France two days later. Concerns at home that England might possibly be invaded by the Germans prevented the full six divisions from being transported to France in early August.

Men of the 1/Leicestershire Regiment on board the SS *Braemar Castle* en route for St Nazaire, September 1914.

Amongst the officers and men of the division there was a real fear that they would arrive too late to join the fight. They had been following the fortunes of the BEF over the retreat from Mons and the advance from the Marne to the Aisne and it was with some relief that orders were received to proceed to Southampton. Strangely, there was little urgency noticeable in getting the three brigades of Major General John Kier's division into line with the BEF, who were at the time crossing the Marne on their way north. Exactly what news had filtered through to Kier's brigades as they marched north towards the Aisne is imprecise but on 16 September Lieutenant Billy Congreve, with the 3rd Rifle Brigade, was still under the impression that the enemy were retiring. It must have come as some surprise to hear that the advance had stalled and instead of joining III Corps as originally planned they were now to be put into general reserve. For once Sir John French had made a strategically sensible decision; there was little point in deploying the division on the left flank with the 4th Division, which is presumably where they were destined. Nevertheless, there had been some discussion at GHQ as to the deployment of Kier's division before it was decided to use the fresh troops as reinforcements for what was now a very tired and depleted BEF; only the divisional artillery brigades would take their place with III Corps. Consequently 16 Brigade were sent to relieve 7 and 9 Brigades above Vailly, 17 Brigade were placed in corps reserve and 18 Brigade went to relieve the hard pressed 1 and 2 Brigades on the extreme of the BEF right flank.

Lieutenant William 'Billy' La Touche Congreve. He was appointed to the staff of the 3rd Division on 21 September and killed on 20 July 1916. Awarded a posthumous VC, he had previously been awarded the DSO and MC.

Attacks of 17 September

On 17 September the Germans launched an attack on the right flank in the pouring rain and 'in considerable strength'. Needham's company of Northamptons were in reserve just above Troyon but were hastily summoned to the firing line, where the battalion was ordered to counter attack:

> We reached the road (Chemin des Dames) and lay down there for a few minutes to get our breath. Then Payker gave the order to fix bayonets and a few minutes later to charge. Over the low bank we went, Payker shouting "Come on, the Cobblers!" and the men cheering like hell. I ran as hard as best I could over the roots with

*my drawn sword in one hand and my revolver in the other,
stumbling and cursing over the roots and expecting every minute
to be tripped up by my sword scabbard! We charged through
heavy rifle and machine gun fire and men were dropping off in
every direction. We got to about thirty yards from the trench we
had passed over on Monday and which was now strongly held. By
now everyone was pretty well blown, and I was thankful when I
saw the whole line throwing themselves down flat.*

With a firing line established, the Northamptons and the KRRC on their
right kept up a continuous fire on the Germans in front of them. After
'what seemed like hours later' Needham was informed that his
company commander, Captain Robert Parker – or Payker to the
company officers – had been killed and he was now in command. Not
only that, said the messenger, but the company of KRRC on his right
had all their officers killed or wounded and he was now in command of
those as well! Sending a runner back to ask for orders, the message
arrived back from Osborne-Smith telling Needham to hold on where he
was and keep up as much fire as possible on the German trench:

*Then suddenly I heard the men shouting "They're surrendering!"
and looking up I saw a line of white flags (or rather white
handkerchiefs or something of the kind tied to the muzzles of
rifles) held up all along the German trench ... I shouted to the
men to cease fire and stop where they were.*

Needham watched in astonished silence as several hundred German

infantrymen left their trenches and began moving
towards A Company where they stood apparently
talking to Captain John Savage and Lieutenant
John Dimmer of the KRRC.

After a few minutes Dimmer and Savage
turned and began walking back to the British line
– the white flags were still in evidence said
Needham:

*To our horror, after they had got about halfway
to us, the Germans opened fire on them and we
saw Savage pitch forward dead, shot in the
back, while Dimmer threw himself down and
started to crawl back to us, eventually reaching
our line all right.*

**Captain John Arkdeen
Savage, 1/Northamptonshire
Regiment. The photo-graph
was taken in 1909 while the
battalion was in India.**

Horrified and unable to take his eyes off the
carnage that was unfolding in front of him was
twenty year-old Second Lieutenant Cosmo
Gordon, a grandson of General Gordon of

Khartoum. Gordon had been gazetted into the battalion in January and was described by Needham as 'a typical cheery, plucky boy straight from Sandhurst'. Needham later wrote that he only realized young Gordon had been hit when 'he pitched forward on his face and yelled out "Oh my God, I'm hit!" He writhed about on the ground in agony and I tried to keep him quiet, while at the same time trying to watch Dimmer and what was going on down the line'.

Corporal John Stennett was witness to the events from the C Company line, where the men had stood up to receive the prisoners:

All of a sudden the front line of Germans fell flat and a second line opened a rapid fire with machine guns and rifles cutting us down like mowing corn. Of 187 which started 8 of us came out, 6 being wounded and two without a scratch, and if it had not been for the Queen's Royal West Surreys we should have been prisoners or perhaps done in, but they took them in hand and cut them up in all directions. Then they had the sauce to show the white flag again but the Queen's ignored it.

Stennett's account was written in England after he had been evacuated with wounds received during the white flag encounter.

But although he confuses his dates, he is correct about the second white flag incident, which he is quite sure the Queen's ignored and

The war artist Fortunino Matania's impression of the white flag incident on the Chemin des Dames that involved the men of A Company, 1/Northamptons.

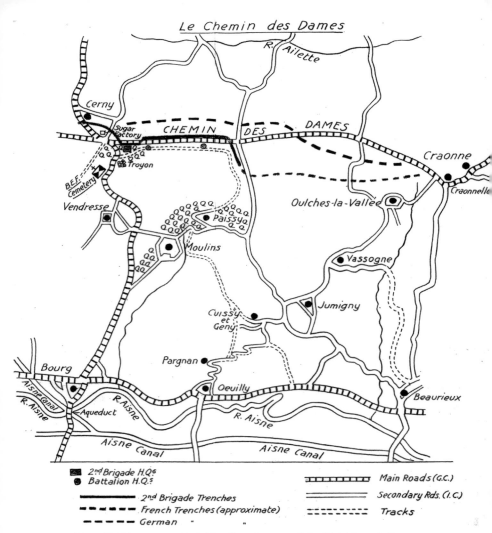

Map 12. Lieutenant Jack Needham's map of the British and German lines on the Chemin des Dames.

opened fire. On this occasion, a short time after the first, another party of Germans approached the Northamptons lines with their hands up. This time there was no discussion and the second group were mown down almost to a man by the Queen's machine guns. Whether this group did wish to genuinely surrender or not will forever remain a mystery but this and other similar incidents did have serious repercussions for some prisoners of war who were treated very badly as a result.

The encounter concluded with the British occupying the trenches evacuated by the Germans, Needham finding the trench 'full of dead

114

and dying Germans', which they proceeded to fill in, 'burying the dead, all of us furious and embittered at having seen Savage and Gordon killed under the white flag like that'. All in all it had been a bad day. It had not been a good day for the Queen's either. Apart from the German counter attack on the Chemin des Dames and the dreadful white flag episode, Cuthbert Avis was aware that earlier in the morning the Moroccans on the right of the battalion had been pushed back by the German *8th Infantry Division* and units of *XII Corps*, which left the Queen's flank unprotected until it was hastily filled by reserves from the British 2 Brigade. To make matters worse, the subsequent French artillery barrage also plastered the Queen's trenches, causing some casualties. Then, writes Avis, 'the commanding officer, Colonel Dawson Warren, met his death by a sniper's bullet and the Adjutant, Captain Charles Wilson, was killed at regimental headquarters near a haystack'. Avis ends his diary on 18 September, having been wounded by a shell splinter and evacuated.

The attacks of 20 September

Whether a conscious decision to concentrate infantry attacks on the right of the BEF's line had been made by the Germans or not, after 19 September it certainly looked as though this was the case. On the left flank, Vailly, Missy and Bucy-le-Long were heavily shelled on a regular basis but no infantry attacks were forthcoming apart from that made on the 3rd Division. The assault began with a diversionary attack on 9 Brigade, who were southwest of Rouge Maison Farm and was dealt with swiftly by the Royal Fusiliers. Any discussion the Germans may have had about counter attacking was probably interrupted by some very accurate shelling by two howitzers from XXX Brigade. The Fusiliers then drove the enemy snipers from the woods to their front and by 1pm peace had once again descended on the line. A similar artillery bombardment had been directed at the 7 Infantry Brigade positions between 8 and 9am that morning and it soon became apparent that the attack on 9 Brigade had been a feint to draw reserves away from the main focus of attack.

In the 7 Brigade firing line were the 2/Royal Irish Rifles and the 1/Wiltshires with the 3/Worcesters in reserve. Leading the attack were *56th* and *64th Infantry Regiments*. The first Lieutenant Alexander Johnstone at 7 Brigade HQ heard of the attack was a message from the Irish Rifles stating they were under heavy attack. Brigade HQ was situated at the time close to the minor road running northeast from Croix Bury on the D925. The events that followed were chronicled in

Johnstone's diary account, which levels a degree of criticism at his brigade commander's use of reserves:

The General [McCracken] *therefore promptly sent up one company of the 2nd South Lancs to their support. This was a mistake, I thought so at the time and still do: the 2nd Irish Rifles, though heavily attacked, had not asked for help yet and were pretty well holding their own. The result was that our reserve of one weak battalion was already diminished by one quarter. Soon after there seemed to be fairly heavy musketry fire in the 1st Wilts lines and the General promptly sent up another company of the 2nd South Lancs. Here again we had merely heard heavy firing so far, and like the 2nd Irish Rifles the 1st Wilts still had a company of the 3rd Worcesters as a local reserve.*

With only two companies of the South Lancs left in reserve, Johnstone bit his tongue and awaited developments. In the meantime German infantry, screened by dense undergrowth, had pushed through a gap in the line between the Worcesters and the Wiltshires and were firing across in enfilade at the Irish and Worcester lines. Initially it looked as if the Germans had finally managed to achieve what they failed to do a week earlier – break through and split II Corps from Haig's I Corp's divisions on the right.

The Germans had obviously got through our line somehow and one did not know what had happened to the 1st Wilts in front. We

Brigade and battalion HQs were often dug into sheltered sites just behind the front line. Pictured is the HQ of 2/KRRC. Note the rudimentary shelter from shellfire, offering little protection from a direct hit.

called up the last company of the 2nd South Lancs, who were in
the cutting just below us, but had great difficulty in getting them
to go forward ... the situation indeed seemed serious, the
Germans were right in our position now, the wood within 150
yards of Brigade HQ was full of German snipers picking off our
men as they showed themselves, they had got a maxim there too
which was doing a lot of damage.

Events turned in favour of the British when a company of 2/South
Staffords from the 2nd Division began working their way up the valley
on the enemy's left flank and a gun from XXIII Brigade RFA opened
fire on the gathering German infantry. 'They got the range first shot',
wrote a relieved Johnstone, 'and had to risk putting a shell into our own
fellows: however as it happened it was the turning point of the day'. At
around 4pm an advance by the Wiltshires, Irish Rifles and Worcesters
finally pushed the enemy back to their own lines, leaving, the Official
History tells us, 'the ground behind littered with his killed and
wounded'. Johnstone stood by his criticism of McCracken:

I am convinced that had we been more careful with our reserves
until we had some idea of the situation, and then given a unit a
definite task such as to clear the wood just N of Brigade HQ, we
should have done much better. As it was we were at one time in
rather a tight corner with only a platoon in reserve and the
Germans within a few yards of Brigade HQ.

The day's fighting had cost 7 Brigade some 400 casualties, most of
which were from 2/South Lancs. The Wiltshire's casualties, although
comparatively light, did include the commanding officer, Lieutenant
Colonel Arthur W Hasted. Hasted was the second commanding officer
in 7 Brigade to be wounded in the space of two days, joining Lieutenant
Colonel Wilkinson Bird of the Irish Rifles, who was badly wounded on
19 September.

1/King's Liverpool Regiment

The attacks on the 2nd Division on the morning of 20 September began
at dawn and fell on the King's Liverpool Regiment's front, east of the
canal in the Braye valley and on the Connaught Rangers, positioned
further to the east on the Beaulne spur. Lieutenant William Synge of the
King's found dawn of 20 September to be wet and misty when they
'were rudely disturbed by the rattle of a machine gun'. Hurriedly
moving his men under cover, he spotted the tell-tale cloud of steam that
issues from the water jacket of the Maxim machine gun, betraying its
position in the strip of wood that ran down to the lock keeper's house.
'We knew the range, and that machine gun was finished off in half a

Sitting just behind the front line is Lieutenant Charles Rolph of the 1/Leicestershire Regiment. Note that Rolph has discarded his service revolver in favour of a Lee Enfield rifle.

minute.' Watching from his company trenches – which were a little above those of C and D Companies – Synge and his men were able to catch the German attack in a deadly crossfire, 'it was exactly like ferreting for rabbits, and I do not think many of those who came out of the wood got back into it again'.

At about 9am the German infantry made a second – more determined – attack:

The attack had now veered round to our right, and we could catch glimpses of the enemy running about on the high ground above. As they were also firing down onto us through the wood, things were by no means pleasant. At this time I was sent back by the Colonel with a message to the second-in-command, who was back on the hill top above Moussy, finding a position onto which we might fall back if the worst came to the worst ... on getting back to the Colonel, who was in the same place, namely where the pathway entered the wood, I found that matters were going very badly indeed.

The Connaughts by this time had been shelled out of their trenches, the German artillery getting the exact range of the forward trenches which, in the words of the war diary, 'made them untenable'. The King's right flank was now dangerously exposed and enemy infantry began firing down on the King's from above, 'for a moment or two we all thought that they were through and that very soon we should be surrounded'. But Synge's qualms were soon dispelled by the arrival of reinforcements in the form of two platoons from B Company of the Highland Light Infantry and six more from the 2/Worcesters. The consequent counter attack captured the first line German trench beyond the Connaughts' positions but elation turned to anguish when the relieving force were ambushed in the woods. There was momentary chaos as the British fell back on A Company of the Kings:

The Colonel, however, refused to retire, and sent me up with a message to the commander of A Company, which was holding the trenches in the wood, to the effect that he must hold out, and there were no more reinforcements. This captain, owing to the thickness of the wood, was very much in the dark as to what was going on, swung his line round slightly so it was facing the crest, and ordered his men to fire rapid fire until further orders into the trees towards the hill-top ... this move, I think, saved the situation, for the Germans began to withdraw.

It had been another close call. Synge was of the opinion that 'had the country been more open, and had they been able to see what they were doing' the Germans would have got right through the British lines and into Moussy, where they would have captured the guns and 'also probably the Brigadier and his staff'.

Casualties
The Official History felt the day belonged to the King's as their casualties did not exceed fifty, but far in excess of that figure was the casualty return from the Highland Light Infantry. After leaving Verneuil to support the Worcesters – who were under attack on the

Beaulne spur – every man from B Company who took part in the counter attack was either killed or wounded. Lieutenant William Lilburn, who led the two platoons of Highlanders, only managed to get back himself after dark with a few of the survivors. The day's fighting cost the Highland Light Infantry three officers killed and two others wounded; they also lost Lieutenant John O'Connell, the battalion's medical officer, who was killed tending the wounded. In the ranks

twenty men were killed, seventy wounded and twenty five missing. Other casualties of the day included Major William Sarsfield, the commanding officer of the Connaughts, who had led the battalion since late August. The shellfire which drove the battalion out of their trenches killed Sarsfield and 22-year-old Second Lieutenant Robert de Stacpoole, the fourth son of the Duke of Stacpoole.

Lieutenant Robert de Stacpoole, Connaught Rangers.

Three other officers were also killed, along with thirty five other ranks killed and wounded. Although not corroborated by the war diary, Sergeant John MacIlwain's diary does give us an indication of the strength of the battalion – despite being reinforced by about 200 officers and men from the special reserve a week earlier – who estimated that the battalion was less than 400 strong at roll call on 21 September.

The attack on the 1st Battalion West Yorkshire Regiment

The 1/West Yorkshires began their relief of the Coldstream after dark on 19 September. Lieutenant Colonel Francis Towsey deployed A and B Companies under Major Alexander Ingles into the firing line along the Chemin des Dames and his remaining two companies into the support trenches, along with the HQ staff.

The troop movements during the relief must have alerted the Germans, as they were fired on shortly after 9pm, which did little more than hone the vigilance of the men in the firing line. But much more was to follow at daybreak.

On the right of the West Yorkshires the North African troops of XVIII Corps were in position on the extreme left of the French Fifth Army. September 20 was another cold day, with heavy showers of hail and rain and it was on the poorly equipped French colonial troops that the first onslaught of the morning fell. The West Yorkshires on

Lieutenant Colonel Francis Towsey, commanding 1/West Yorkshires.

their left reported heavy shellfire from about 4am onwards and at 4.14am some Moroccan troops began leaving their positions. Although they were encouraged to return, the Yorkshire's right flank was immediately put under pressure and became increasingly vulnerable in the face of the wavering Moroccan troops. With this in mind, Towsey sent an officer's patrol under Lieutenant Thomas Meautys out to his right in order to get a fuller picture of what exactly was taking place. Meautys and his men confirmed Towsey's worst fears; the Moroccan troops on his right flank were in no position to contain a resolute German attack and appeared still to be in some disorder. Towsey had no choice but to deploy one company to protect his right.

Private Charles Rainbird was with D Company:

As dawn was breaking this morning, there occurred one of those hellish mistakes which occur in every war. We saw through the half light a large body of men evidently retiring on our right. Our Colonel ordered my Company 'D' to swing round so as to cover their retirement if they should prove to be allies. After advancing about 200 yards we saw that they were allies (Zouaves) when, to our horror they suddenly turned and opened fire on us. Oh God, it was awful, everyone of us exposed to a raking fire and no cover; they had evidently mistaken us for the enemy. My mates were falling all over the place and there was 37 killed in less than two minutes. Naturally our boys opened fire on them, in spite of the CO's shout of "Don't fire!" I dropped one fellow as he was in the act of firing, then we received the order to retire.

In the confusion of the early morning a party of Moroccan troops had opened fire on the Yorkshires as they moved into position, an incident that underlined the delicate nature of the French positions and the men holding them. After this the line appeared to settle down and there was a pause before the second German attack was made sometime after 10am. On this occasion the West Yorkshires were ready for anything and easily checked the attacking enemy infantry and for a while it appeared as if the Moroccan infantry had regained their composure. But this attack was a precursor to the next more determined assault.

The next attack began at about 12.30pm under the cover of a violent rainstorm. This time the Moroccans were thrown back again. Towsey and Lieutenant Meautys both went forward to the firing line to see what was happening – returning a few minutes later with Meautys mortally wounded. According to Captain P H Lowe, who was with D Company, the advanced line of the West Yorkshires was on the forward slope of the hill and composed of a succession of rifle pits, which were unconnected by any communication trenches:

Map 13. A 1917 French trench map showing the French positions on the Chemin des Dames on the extreme right of what was the British sector in 1914. The trench lines to the left of the crossroads are approximately where the 1/West Yorkshires were positioned on 20 September.

The trench here was very badly sited, there being dead ground to the front, though the field of fire to the flanks was good. There was no room in the trench for a number of my men, but there were in many places craters made from shell fire ... we beat off comparatively easily two attacks. Then the Germans massed in the dead ground in front. From here they tried to advance by rushes in small bodies. This was more difficult to stop. In the meantime our casualties had been heavy and particularly from machine guns and shrapnel, which was continually traversing our trenches. Near midday two catastrophes took place. The French went, leaving our flank exposed and a short heavy storm of rain turned the ground into a quagmire. Ammunition was being

122

collected *from the wounded with the result that all the rifles begun to jam.*

Lowe describes how there were only four rifles in his pit that were serviceable and the bayonets on each had been smashed by enemy fire and the bolts on two of the weapons were only able to operate with the help of an entrenching tool:

It appeared to me that the German final effort could only be met with a counter-attack. To be prepared, I endeavoured to find out the officers and NCOs who were still effective. On the right it was reported there were none. The men began to get somewhat disheartened. It was impossible to send any message to the rear. At the very moment the Germans were about to advance, a man about 40 yards on my right began to waver. As soon as I got up to deal with the situation I was hit.

Realizing the need for support, Towsey sent a runner to Brigade HQ at Paissy to ask for assistance.

But the gap left by the retreating French infantry had given the German infantry the opportunity they needed and as the front companies were overwhelmed, the German infantry took possession of the British firing line. The Official History tells us they charged and 'swept the front companies into captivity', but in truth, there were few survivors, and only those who were taken captive knew the exactness of what actually happened.

The first Lieutenant Colonel Towsey knew of the disaster that had befallen his battalion was at 1.30pm when a runner – sent back from

French colonial infantry.

the firing line – brought the news that the companies in the front line had been captured and the Germans were advancing. Gathering together the remnants of the men in the support trenches, Towsey advanced at the head of his men into a hail of fire from his front and right flank. The war diary recorded the inevitable outcome:

> C Company and HQ Company at once advanced towards the front trenches in order, if possible, to save the companies in the firing line; they fixed bayonets and advanced at the double but were met with a heavy fire from the front and right flank. Fire was opened to the front and two platoons turned to the right. The order was then given to retire back to the trench and the original line was again occupied. Owing to this position offering a poor field of fire, the CO decided to retire on to Paissy Hill and connect up with the cavalry on our right.

The retirement of the Yorkshires had peeled open the British line and now the Durham Light Infantry – who were holding the line to the left of the West Yorkshires – came under a heavy enfilade fire. Their situation was not eased until the arrival of the 2nd Battalion Nottinghamshire and Derbyshire Regiment (Sherwood Foresters). The Foresters were in reserve to the north of Troyon, sheltered in the steep sided valley that ran down to Vendresse. As they moved across the head of the valley a German column was seen escorting the West Yorkshire prisoners – including Private Charles Rainbird – who had survived the morning's fighting. Devoid of any cover and with men dropping left and right, the Foresters retook the West Yorkshires trenches at the point of the bayonet, driving out the enemy infantry.

In the meantime 2 Cavalry Brigade was arriving in force with a company of the Royal Sussex. The 4/Dragoon Guards, led by Major

Paissy village. It was from here that 2 Cavalry Brigade and the Royal Sussex Regiment launched their counter attack to regain the trench lines on the Chemin des Dames.

Tom Bridges, dismounted below the ridge, where Bridges – never one to avoid getting into action – was soon running ahead of his men:

> *I got on ahead and, jumping off my horse, told my trumpeter to wait for the squadron and tell Hornby to dismount and look for my signals. I ran on up to the crown of the hill, which was bare stubble, and seemed quite deserted until I saw a German officer's helmeted head coming up the other side. I saw him wave to his men, and I did the same to mine, giving the signal to double. We met the Picklehaubers almost face to face and standing up poured rapid fire into them which put them to flight. A second squadron came up on our right and we occupied some shallow rifle pits previously dug by the infantry.*

When the Dragoon Guards went into dismounted action, Trooper Ben Clouting's job was to stay with the horses, but on this occasion 'the older troopers were quite happy to let the likes of me go instead'. Clouting was soon running up the slope after Tom Bridges:

> *We dropped into small scoops made by some recently departed infantry. It was such a beautiful clear day as the Germans came on, packed together, hundreds of them, marching four deep and at a distance of some eleven hundred yards. They were coming down the far slope of a valley, marching through agricultural fields, as we opened up with our fifteen – rounds – a-minute fire. The vision was perfect. I could see Germans toppling over as the rest came relentlessly on, but with our artillery pounding away, the Germans could only take so much. All of a sudden they turned and bolted back up the valley.*

With the remnants of the West Yorkshires and the Moroccan infantry 'in their blue and silver jackets and red trousers' now rallied and advancing uphill, the cavalrymen's charge and rapid fire had successfully turned the approaching German infantry. By 4.30pm all the Yorkshires' trenches had been retaken and the 9/Lancers – who were sent to entrench a position at the rear of the Moroccans – were firmly in place to 'dissuade them from bolting' again.

With the infantry now back in the trenches and a degree of normalcy restored, the cavalry retired to Paissy. The West Yorkshires' war diarist is 'certain that the Germans advanced under the cover of a white flag' on the right flank, a view that is not supported by Captain Lowe's account of the action – which was completed two years later in 1917, after he was transferred to neutral Switzerland. In his evidence he makes no mention of a white flag incident taking place – which is not to say it did not occur. Lowe's account tells us the line was already beginning to waver before he was hit and, in the absence of officers and

NCOs to steady the line, it is highly probable that the front line companies did indeed retire in confusion. In the West Yorkshires' defence, although they were regulars, they were unseasoned troops who had been put into the front line without the benefit of more experienced men alongside them and, if indeed a white flag ruse was used against them, one can understand how they may have been taken in by it. Later in the war newly arrived battalions would spend a period of probation in the trenches along with more experienced troops to enable them to acclimatize to the local conditions and practices.

The scale of the calamity that had overtaken the West Yorkshires on their introduction to front line duty was enormous. As to who saved the day on 20 September, this is still a subject of some debate. The 2 Cavalry Brigade claim their counter attack was responsible for rallying the French and British infantry – which indeed it did – but full credit must go to the magnificent attack by the Sherwood Foresters that took the front line trenches, albeit at a terrible cost. The battalion lost four officers killed and eight wounded together with forty other ranks killed and 140 wounded. Yet it was the West Yorkshires who suffered most heavily. At roll call on 21 September it became apparent that apart from eight officers killed and two others wounded – including the commanding officer – seven other officers were missing. Amongst the ranks, seventy one were known to have been killed and 110 wounded but 436 were posted as missing, many of whom had been taken prisoner. It had been a very severe baptism of fire for the battalion in what was their first day of action.

At Troyon – after less than three weeks since landing at St Nazaire – Major Godfrey Lang took command of what was left of the battalion – five officers and 250 men. When the Loyal North Lancs took over the West Yorkshires' trenches, Lieutenant James Hyndson was very conscious that they were 'still full of their dead, and it was almost impossible to dig in places without coming on dead bodies'; a scenario that would be all too common in the years of trench warfare that lay ahead.

Douglas Haig was particularly critical of the West Yorkshires and of Lieutenant Colonel Towsey himself. According to his diary account, Haig tells us he was informed by Brigadier General de Lisle that 'the West Yorkshires left their trenches and ran back to Paizy [sic] village, headed apparently by the colonel of the battalion'. Not only that, but he went on to say:

This is the worst incident of which I have heard during this campaign. I do not know Lt.Col. Towsey but in view of the high character which he holds it may be well to give him another chance, but I recommend that he and his battalion be strongly rebuked and that they are told that it rests with them to regain the good name and reputation which our infantry holds, and which they may have by their conduct on the 20th forfeited.

The attacks of 25/26 September

There were several half-hearted attacks on 2 Brigade and against the left of the French XVIII Corps during the morning of 26 September, which were quite easily beaten off, but it was against the frontage occupied by the 1/South Wales Borderers on the Mont Faucon spur that the most serious attack occurred. The battalion held a line running across the spur with a large quarry situated almost at mid-point.The steep sides of the spur, which fell down towards Vendresse on the right, were thickly wooded. At dawn a large force of some 1,200 German infantry from the *21st* and *25th Infantry Divisions* of *XVIII Corps*

A page from the journal of Captain Guy Ward of the 1/SWB describing the events of 26 September.

PENPERGWM LODGE.
Nr ABERGAVENNY.

to get to the Detached Post when heavy firing commences from the direction of the left of the Battalion Line (D.Coy). When we get to the D.P. find them under fire. We relieve the right trench & move over to do the same for the left, and as we go over to it, see the men of the right trench retiring, caused by D.Coy post being driven in. This allows the Germans to get into the wood & so brings the left of us under fire. We form up on a bank & prepare to hold it. Leaving Stewart in charge I go back to the Battalion & on the way ask the Welch who were in reserve for help, they send a Platoon to Stewart.

On returning to my old Coy H.Q. I find Bn H.Q. arrived there and my Nos 3 & 4 Platoons under W.C.C. acting as reserve. Coker returns from a job he was doing for the C.O. while I had been away. No. 3 Platoon goes up to T.O.L. (he now has ... of mine.)

attacked the battalion. Lieutenant Charles Paterson thought it to be 'the most ghastly day' of his life:

> *At 4.15am the Germans attacked. Main attack apparently against my regiment, which is on the left of our line. D and A Companies in the trenches. B and C hustled up in support, and soon the whole place alive with bullets. News comes that they [Germans] are trying to work their way round our left.*

Captain Guy Ward, commanding C Company, remembered getting word that D Company had retired to the shelter of the quarry:

> *This allows the Germans to get into the wood and so bring the lot of us under fire. We form up on a bank and prepare to hold it. Leaving Stewart [Lieutenant Charles Stewart] in charge I go back to the battalion and on the way ask the Welsh, who were in reserve for help, they send a platoon to Stewart ... News comes that Welby [Major Glynne Welby, OC D Company] is killed and Prichard [Lieutenant William Prichard] is wounded. Curgenven [Captain Victor Curgenven] is sent to take command of D Company.*

D Company were clearly taking the brunt of the attack. Charles Paterson was with HQ Company when he heard the news the Germans had broken through the line and apparently got into D Company's lines in the quarry – which formed the centre of the battalion's defences. For a while there was confusion, compounded by Major Anthony Reddie, the battalion's second-in-command, who brought in the disturbing news that C and D Companies had surrendered which, if true, would precipitate a general retirement back towards Vendresse. Guy Ward was sent up by Lieutenant Colonel Bertram Collier to find out exactly what was happening and report back:

> *As far as I could make out what happened was D Company had a line of trenches in front of the quarry and by night several sentries in advance of the trenches. Their custom was to withdraw as soon as it was light enough for the sentries in the trenches to see. As soon as the sentries fell back this morning, the Germans, who evidently had been assembling during the night, followed close behind them and got their machine guns and snipers in position before those in the trenches realized that there were more than just the sentries moving in front of them. The men in the trenches must have been quickly wiped out and the Germans advanced to the quarry. I cannot make out if they actually entered the quarry, I think not as C Company appeared on the scene with fixed bayonets at which the Germans fell back. Curgenven told*

me they advanced at the charge but did not get into them. There were no German dead in the quarry.

For the remainder of the morning the Borderers held their own, not needing to call on the 18 Brigade reinforcements that were on stand-by.

At 11.30am the German infantry – realizing their attack had failed – began to withdraw under the cover of their artillery batteries on the Chemin des Dames. It was the moment the British gunners had been waiting for; as the German infantry became visible in the upper Chivy valley, the gunners opened fire, inflicting heavy casualties on the hapless Germans. We have no definite indication of the damage inflicted in the enemy during their retirement but the Official History suggests the number of enemy killed alone 'must have exceeded the total casualties of the British'.

The British casualties recorded in the I Corps War Diary amounted to six officers and 423 other ranks killed, six officers and ninety one other ranks wounded and 110 missing, the vast majority of whom were subsequently found to have been killed. By far the largest number of dead and wounded came from the South Wales Borderers.

Many of the men killed in action on the Aisne have no known graves and are commemorated on the La Ferté-sous-Jouarre memorial.

1st Battalion Cameron Highlanders

For the 1/Cameron Highlanders 25 September was described by the regimental historian as 'a day of sudden and crippling disaster'. The German shell fire which greeted the dawn that morning began falling on the Cameron Highlanders' positions on the Beaulne spur at around 6.00am. The battalion's trenches were a series of unconnected shallow rifle pits, each capable of holding a section of six to seven men.

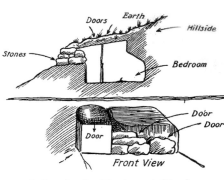

A drawing by Lieutenant Charles Paterson the Adjutant of the 1/South Wales Borderers of his dugout on the Beaulne spur.

Directly behind D Company's forward trenches was a large cave which was being used as Battalion

129

Officer casualties of the Cameron Highlanders pictured before the war. Apart from James Matheson all those circled were killed on the Aisne: back row – Lieutenant N C Cameron, Lieutenant J S Matheson (wounded and rescued by Private Tollerton), 2/Lieutenant N K Cameron and 2/Lieutenant H W Cameron. Middle row – Captain A G Cameron, Captain D Miers and Captain A Mackintosh.

HQ – another similar cave nearby was sheltering some of the officers and men of C Company. In command of the battalion was Captain Douglas Miers. Some half an hour after the bombardment began Douglas Miers was wounded by a shell splinter and returned to the HQ Cave to have his wounds attended to by Lieutenant John Crocket, the battalion medical officer. Sending word to Captain Allan Cameron – the next senior officer in the battalion – to take command, Miers waited in the cave to hand-over officially to Cameron. His departure for the dressing station at Verneuil was delayed by another salvo of enemy shells and it was while he remained in the shelter of the cave that two large shells hit the cave, one directly on top and the other at the entrance. The whole structure was brought down, entombing the twenty nine occupants.

This was another serious blow to the battalion. Not only had Miers and Allan Cameron been killed in the falling rubble but three other officers, John Crocket, Lieutenant Napier Cameron and the battalion Adjutant, Lieutenant Kenneth Meiklejohn, were also killed, along with the RSM George Burt. There were four survivors, including Bandsmen Rosser and Ursell, who escaped unscathed and Corporal Mitchell, who was pulled out alive but badly crushed. Command fell to Captain Ewen Brodie, who was one of only two officers left alive in the battalion. Three days later the new draft of officers and men – sent out to replace the losses of 14 September – arrived with the new commanding officer, Lieutenant Colonel Douglas McEwen.

McEwen's arrival on the Aisne on 28 September found the British positions almost exactly the same as they had been at nightfall on 14 September. The morning had begun with the usual mist that on the 2/Coldstream frontage at Cour de Soupir Farm allowed a small patrol of three men to approach the forward German trenches unseen. Suddenly the mist lifted, placing the three men in range of enemy rifle fire; two were shot down and the third escaped with only a graze to return to the safety of the Coldstream front line. Not waiting for darkness to bring in the two wounded men, Private Frederick Dobson crawled out under heavy fire across the exposed ground to find one of the men dead and the other badly wounded but alive. Having applied first aid he returned to his company trenches to collect a stretcher. Accompanied by Corporal Brown, the two men successfully brought the wounded man back to safety. Dobson was awarded the Victoria Cross and Brown the Distinguished Conduct Medal for their selfless act. Dobson's VC was the second that had been awarded to the Coldstream since war was declared.

The move to Flanders

By early October both sides were exhausted, frontal attacks – no matter how gallantly led or undertaken– had proved ineffectual and the two sides appeared content for the time being to throw high explosive at each other. However, towards the end of September discussions had begun between Sir John French and General Joffre which focussed on the BEF moving to the extreme left of the allied line in order to be closer to their lines of communication and link up with the 7th Division, which had landed at Ostend. Joffre agreed and on the night of 1 October 1914 the carefully concealed move of British troops began. The first to move were the cavalry followed by II Corps and by 14 October the last man of the BEF had left the Aisne trench lines. The First Battle of Ypres was but

Private Frederick Dobson.

days away and by the end of the year the regular army that embarked for France in August would be all but gone.

The Aisne legacy

The sluggish allied advance towards the Aisne in September 1914 allowed the German army time to reinforce and dig in on the Chemin des Dames. Thus the high ground to the north of the Aisne valley oversaw the beginnings of a trench based battle which was largely dictated by the tactical nature of the fighting. On the Chemin des Dames the Germans had found a position they could defend effectively and in order to hold it they resorted to the spade. In response the Anglo-French armies that were attempting, unsuccessfully, to evict them with frontal assaults and outflanking movements found themselves digging parallel positions opposite their adversaries. As the process repeated itself, the lines of trenches gradually moved to the north and west as both sides attempted to get round the open western flank and end the war with a final battle. The trench system that became known as the Western Front was created by the flanking attacks that were forced upon both sides by the stalemate on the Aisne. The picturesque rolling hills and valleys of the Aisne had unwittingly given birth to a positional warfare that would eventually create the 400 mile Western Front from Nieuwpoort on the Belgian coast to the Swiss border.

Although neither side envisaged a war conducted from fixed positions, it was the Germans who had the advantage of position and had the choice of selecting the Chemin des Dames ridge as their line of defence. Not only that, but they had a ready supply of trench warfare equipment to hand. Barbed wire, spades, duckboards and trench mortars were available in quantity, catching the British and French armies on the back foot with their lack of trench resources. German artillery was distinctly more powerful and used to a much greater effect than the inadequate artillery support offered by the Allied armies. The intensity and accuracy of the German gunners, which had taken GHQ by surprise, was undoubtedly another reason behind Operational Order No 27 from Sir John French on 16 September, which instructed his divisions to dig in and hold their positions against German attacks. Sir John was correct in thinking trenches enabled both sides to hold ground and protect themselves against shell fire but with no subsequent orders being issued until 1 October – when the British withdrawal from the Aisne began – the BEF was left without direction from its commander-in-chief. It was in these two weeks – when the spade became the most sought after weapon in the valley – that trench warfare is said to have become a reality.

Chapter Eight

THE TOURS

Using the Guide and Advice to Visitors

In order fully to appreciate a battleground and what took place on and around it, it is essential to get out on the ground and walk or bike in the footsteps of history. This guide has been written with that purpose in mind and in the touring section there are several walks/bike routes that should cater for all levels of fitness. For those who lack time, or wish to get an overall impression of the area, two routes are included that focus on the car as the principal method of transport.

There is plenty of advice available for walkers and bikers in other editions of the Battleground Europe series and while I do not propose to reiterate it all in this volume, I will underline the need to exercise good sense as a guiding principle when going off the beaten track. The Aisne valley in particular is sparsely populated and battlefield tourists can quickly find themselves away from all vestiges of civilization, with little in the way of shelter or refreshment available. Once above the collection of small villages that run along the valley floor, the flat tops of the numerous spurs that run down from the Chemin des Dames can appear featureless and remote, even more so on a misty morning when visibility is restricted. It goes without saying that suitable footwear and clothing should be the order of the day. The Aisne is often blessed with sunshine, particularly in the summer months, and sun cream, a suitable hat and plenty of liquid should be included in your day-sac. Other items I have found to be useful are a good pair of binoculars, a small first aid kit and a decent map case and a compass.

Finally, a word of warning about wandering into caves. On the Aisne you will inevitably come across some of the numerous caves that dot the landscape; many of these caves were used by the succession of troops of both sides that found themselves fighting in the area over the course of the war. Exploration of these cavities without the benefit of expert guidance can be dangerous and should not be undertaken without appropriate equipment. It is very tempting to explore with the aid of a torch but these caves are potentially dangerous and battlefield tourists who enter them do so at their own risk entirely. There is another more obvious danger from battlefield debris in the form of spent rounds and unexploded shells. Although not as numerous on the Aisne as they are on other parts of the Western Front, they still exist and it is not uncommon to find old ordnance piled up at various points awaiting collection by a French army bomb disposal unit. Please leave them where they are; they are still dangerous and unstable, despite their age.

Maps

For an overall view of the area the IGN 09 1:100,000 Carte de Promenade is probably the most useful for the car tours. For walkers the area is covered by two of the IGN1:25,000 Top 25 Série Bleue maps, 2611E – Braine and 2711O – Soissons.

Travel to the Aisne

Travel time from Calais to the Chemin des Dames is approximately three hours driving depending on where you are intending to base yourself. Calais to Cerny-en-Laonnois is 149 miles using the A26 from Calais and two thirds of the journey is on the motorway itself. By far the quickest passage across the Channel is via the Tunnel at Folkstone, the thirty five minutes travelling time comparing favourably with the longer ferry journey from Dover. Whether your choice of route is over or under the Channel, early booking well in advance is always recommended if advantage is to be taken of the cheaper fares.

Driving abroad is not the expedition it was years ago and most battlefield visitors these days may well have already made the journey several times. However, if this is the first time you have ventured on French roads there are one or two common sense rules to take into consideration. Ensure your vehicle is properly insured and covered by suitable breakdown insurance; if in doubt contact your insurer, who will advise you. There are also a number of compulsory items to be carried by motorists that are required by French law. These include your driving licence and vehicle registration documents, a warning triangle, a *Conformité Européenne* (CE) approved fluorescent safety vest, headlamp beam convertors and the visible display of a GB plate. Whereas some modern cars have built in headlamp convertors and many have a GB plate incorporated into the rear number plate, French law also requires the vehicle to be equipped with a first aid kit, a fire extinguisher and a breath test kit. If you fail to have these available there are some hefty on the spot fines for these motoring offences if caught driving without them. Most, if not all, of these items can be purchased at the various outlets at the Tunnel and the channel port at Dover and on board the ferries themselves.

Driving on the 'wrong side of the road' can pose some challenges. Here are three tips that the author has always found useful:

When driving in France on single carriageway roads try to stop at petrol stations on the right hand side of the road. It is much more

134

natural then to continue driving on the right hand side of the road after you leave. Leaving a garage or supermarket is often the time when you find yourself naturally turning onto the wrong side of the road.

2. Take your time! Don't rush! If you rush your instinct may take over and your instinct is geared to driving on the left.

3. Pay particular care on roundabouts. A lot of French drivers do not and appear to use indicators rarely. Navigators remember to look at the signs anti-clockwise and drivers remember that the danger is coming from the left.

On a personal note it is always advisable to ensure your E1 11 Card is valid in addition to any personal accident insurance you may have and have a supply of any medication that you may be taking at the time.

Where to stay

Battlefield visitors to the Aisne valley have the choice of staying in the larger urban conurbations of Laon or Soissons, in the valley itself or in the surrounding area. The valley does not have a great deal of choice when it comes to accommodation but the author has stayed on several occasions at the two star Auberge de la Valley at 6, Rue d'Oeuilly, Bourg-et-Comin, run by the Dardene family. The hotel is clean and comfortable and boasts a good restaurant and is within walking distance of the aqueduct over the river used by the 1st Division on 13 September 1914. Further to the east along the D 925, Tony and Thierry Bridier have converted an old barn by the river into what I consider to be a good quality bed and breakfast establishment at 6 Impasse des Prés, Cuiry-lès-Chaudardes. The four star Hôtel du Golf at Chamouille in the Ailette valley is close to the Aisne Center Parc resort which is situated on the Lac de l'Ailette. The Centre Parc resort, is extremely handy for visitors wishing to combine a family holiday with visits to the battlefield. To the south of the river, Antoine and Sophie Hubert offer, in my opinion, a good class of accommodation at La Carrière l'Evêcque Farm, just north of Septmonts. This has an added attraction in that it was used as a casualty collection station and ambulance park by the BEF during the Aisne campaign of 1914.

Laon, as you would expect, has a number of hotels and bed and breakfast locations including an Ibis and Campanile located in the business district just outside

Laon Cathedral

the town centre, while the more central three star Hotel de la Bannière de France is to be found at 11 Rue Franklin-Roosevelt.

There are a number of quite decent restaurants in the centre to cater for all tastes. The medieval hill top town also boasts a very grand cathedral and was the German regional headquarters from 1914. It was here that General Hans von Zwehl reported to von Bülow after leaving Maubeuge with the *VII Reserve Corps* en route to the Chemin des Dames.

The Soissons Memorial to the Missing, commemorating those lost from the British IX Corps and XXII Corps in 1918. Note the centre sculpture of three soldiers, which are the work of Eric Kennington.

Further west, Soissons also has a remarkably fine cathedral which is situated a short distance from the Soissons Memorial on the Rue de la Bannière. The Memorial commemorates nearly 4,000 officers and men who died during the Battles of the Aisne and the Marne in 1918 and who have no known grave. Soissons has a good selection of hotels and restaurants including a Campanile and the Best Western Hôtel des Francs in the centre.

Camping is always an option and the area has a number of sites, including the municipal campsite just outside Soissons (details on the Soissons municipal website http://uk.ville-soissons.fr) and Camping de la Pointe at Bourg-et-Comin (www.camping-aisne.com), where I can recommend the swimming pool and the restaurant.

With children in mind

Combining battlefield tourism with a family holiday can be problematic, particularly when young children have had enough of visiting Great War sites and begin questioning the rationale behind yet another visit to yet another cemetery! One option is to combine a stay at the Center Parcs (http://www.centerparcs.fr) venue in the Ailette valley with some battlefield tourism, or, at the very least, to take advantage of a day ticket for the Aqua Mundo water feature in the Parc for yourself and the children. The author can personally vouch for the quality of the water slides! A visit to the Caverne du Dragon (www.caverne-du-dragon.fr), which has a museum and a cafe, offering wonderful views over the Aisne valley, also goes down well with children and adults alike, as do the variety of activities centred on Fort Condé (www.fortdeconde.com). The fort offers numerous activities for

136

children including a family game involving discovering clues scattered around the fort. Outside the fort there are a number of circular walks/bike rides, a picnic area and cafe. Take a picnic and spend a day there exploring the area and the myriad of passages inside the fort.

The car tours have been designed to give you the opportunity to explore all the main features of the BEF sector. The numbers in the text **(1)** correspond with the circular numerics used on the maps. There are numerous opportunities to get out of the vehicle and stretch your legs and I would urge you to do so. This is a beautiful part of France and the views can be quite stunning. Please bear in mind that both car tours direct you along some minor roads that are often narrow and lack passing places, vehicles much larger than a minibus may have difficulty and farm machinery is always a possibility. As with similar parts of rural France, refreshment stops are few and far between and a picnic will often be the best lunchtime solution.

CAR TOUR 1 – THE LEFT FLANK

Start: Vénizel bridge
Finish: Vailly bridge
Distance: 25 miles/32 kilometres

This tour covers part of the left flank of the BEF where the 4th Division crossed the Aisne at Vénizel and moved north to occupy the edge of the high ground above Bucy-le-Long. From Bucy the tour heads north into what was German held territory in 1914, straying briefly into the French Sixth Army sector before visiting Vregny, Chivres-Val and the Fort de Condé. At Missy-sur-Aisne we cross onto the south side of the river in order to visit the German held bridge at Condé. The tour concludes with a visit to Rouge Maison Farm before finishing at the bridge where the 3rd Division crossed the river.

We begin on the south bank of the River Aisne at Vénizel in the small car park **(1)** by the old level crossing, which is some fifty metres from the road bridge.

From the car park walk down to the river bank where you will find the concrete abutments of the original bridge crossed by the 4th Division on the wet night of 12 September.

If you look carefully across to the far bank the bridge abutments can be seen nestling amongst the undergrowth. Return to your vehicle and cross the bridge using the D95 which will take you across the flat water meadows to Bucy-le-Long. It was across this ground that *Hauptmann Walter Bloem*, from his vantage point on the Chivres spur, observed the 2/Lancashire Fusiliers advancing in artillery formation. At the

The abutments of the 1914 Bridge at Vénizel.

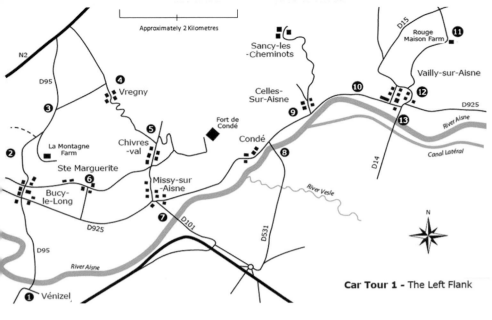

roundabout continue straight ahead following the D95 over two crossroads until you reach the T-junction with the Rue Chemin des Dames. Turn left and follow the road steeply uphill to the communal cemetery **(2)** where there is parking. For a description of the cemetery see **Route 1 – La Montagne Farm**.

From the cemetery continue uphill with woods on either side, taking the next turning on the right to La Montagne Farm. Beware, this is a very sharp turning and will take you to the southern edge of the spur overlooking the Aisne river.

On a clear day you can get fine views through the trees of the Vénizel bridge and the ground

La Montagne Farm.

crossed by the 4th Division. Retrace your steps and stop about 200 metres from the road junction. Look across to the right over the open fields, to the east. This is the approximate line the British battalions held during the campaign. From where you are standing the line continued behind you to the south west, to point 151, where it joined up with the French Sixth Army.

Continue north on the D95 until you reach the next crossroads **(3)**. Turn right here and drive along the narrow road until La Montagne Farm becomes visible to your right and stop. This is the view the attacking Germans would have had of the British positions north of the farm. This minor road crosses La Grande Piéce to arrive at a T-junction

139

with the D53. Turn right and follow the road down to Vregny **(4)**. The village was held by the Germans in 1914 and despite the efforts of the BEF on 13 September, Vregny remained in German hands during the campaign. It was later taken by the French and used as a jumping off point on 16 April for the Nivelle offensive in 1917. Totally destroyed during the war, the forty or so private houses were rebuilt, but today the village has a population of less than a hundred.

Once in the village you will come to a T-junction opposite a large farm. To your left is the village war memorial. Turn right and continue downhill, passing the rebuilt Château Vregny on your left, to the junction with the D423 at Chivres-Val **(5)**. Turn left again along the minor road and follow the signs for the Fort de Condé.

The entrance to the Fort de Condé.

The fort was built as part of the Sere de Rivières system, which was constructed with the intention of defending the border following the Treaty of Frankfurt of 1871 which ended the Franco-Prussian War of 1870 -1871. Its usefulness was short lived. Rendered obsolete by the evolution of modern weaponry, it was decommissioned in 1912. In September 1914 it was occupied by the Germans and during the BEF campaign played host to numerous heavy artillery batteries and a searchlight unit, remaining a thorn in the side of the British and French until April 1917 when the Nivelle offensive was launched. In October 1917, the commander-in-chief of the

Part of the interior of the Fort de Condé.

American Expeditionary Force, General John Pershing, together with General Louis Franchet d'Esperey came to observe the battlefield from the fort. Needless to say the fort was returned to German occupation after the Blücher-Yorck offensive of 1918 until 7 August when the German army finally left the Aisne. The fort was disarmed after the war before being abandoned in 1927.

After leaving the fort return to Chivres-Val. Until 1921 the village

140

The CWGC plot at Ste Marguerite Churchyard Cemetery.

was called Chivres-sur-Aisne and was held by *52 Infantry Regiment* in September and October 1914. After the French took the village it was used as another jumping off point during the Nivelle offensive. From the village turn take the D958 – signposted Bucy-le-Long – for a little over a kilometre until you see the church at Ste Marguerite **(6)** on the right. You are now in the Rue de Georges Guynemer, named after the famous French aviator killed in Belgium on 11 September 1917. Park near the church to visit the cemetery.

Of the six burials here, five are Lancashire Fusiliers. **Private William Gratrix** was killed on 13 September and **Corporal Edgar Slough** a day later. **Private James Murphy** and **Second Lieutenant John Paulson** were killed on 17 September. Two men were recorded being killed attempting to bring in the wounded Paulson after he had been hit by shellfire, one of these may have been **Private Murphy**. **Private Christopher Brooks**, from Whittle Woods near Chorley, was killed on 25 September. The church was one of the early dressing stations established by units of 10 and 11/Field Ambulance and these men may well have died of their wounds here. On the wall of the churchyard is an information panel devoted to three French aircrew who were killed in May 1940.

Return to your vehicle and continue on the minor road directly opposite the church – Rue Moulin des Roches – do not be alarmed when the road surface changes, you will soon arrive at the junction with the D925. Straight ahead is the track leading down to the approximate location where 17/Field Company ferried 14 and 15 Brigade across the river in rafts at the Moulin des Roches and where the 2/Bridging Train's pontoon bridge was constructed. Turn left and, just before you enter

141

Missy, you will see a signpost to La Biza Farm on the right. This is where **Brigadier General Gleichen** and the staff of 15 Brigade established their headquarters. At the crossroads with the D101 turn right to cross the road bridge **(7)** over the Aisne. There is a convenient parking spot on the right after you cross the bridge. Walk back to the bridge but take care, as this stretch of road can be busy.

From the pedestrian walkway on the bridge look across to your right to where a line of woods borders the river. This is where **Captain Jim Pennyman** was commanding D Company, which was effectively pinned down by the volume of fire from the high ground you can see to the north. Reference to the sketch map he drew will be useful here.

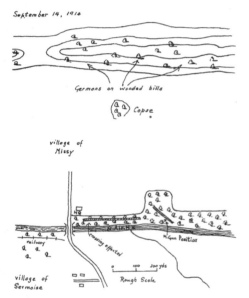

It was when the Germans began threatening the right flank of the Borderers that Pennyman moved 18-year-old **Lieutenant Gilbert Amos** and his platoon to cover that flank. Amos was killed shortly afterwards. This was where the battalion medical officer, **Captain Robert Dolbey**, crossed the river in a raft to join the men in the woods. Pennyman was hit whilst in the woods some time later and ferried back to the southern bank after dark.

Return to your vehicle and carry on along the D101. Just before the road goes under the E46 turn left along the minor road which will take you to a large roundabout. Take the fourth exit signposted Chassemy and follow the D141/D531, which will take you over the River Vesle and to the Condé bridge. As you approach the Condé bridge **(8)** note the prominence of the Chivres spur up ahead with the Fort de Condé hidden amongst the trees. The long straight approach to the bridge was guarded by German machine guns and considered too perilous to take in a frontal assault; a notion probably fostered by the cavalry skirmish of 13 September. On this occasion the bridge was approached by a patrol of 4/Hussars and met by a hail of machine gun fire, which resulted in the loss of a trooper. Sent out twice more, each patrol continued to take casualties from well directed

142

machine gun fire. Thereafter it was never again put to the test and thus remained in German hands for the duration of the campaign.

Cross the bridge and turn right at the junction. You will soon arrive at the turning on the left signposted Celles-sur-Aisne and Sancy-les-Cheminots **(9)**. Here you have the choice of continuing straight on to Vailly or taking a short diversion to visit two sites that are closely associated with the French occupancy of the area. The first stop is the communal cemetery at Celles-sur-Aisne, which is signposted once you enter the village. As you enter the cemetery look to your left to find the grave of 29-year-old **Lieutenant Jean Fernand Balossy**, who was killed on 10 May 1917 fighting with the 219th Regiment of Artillery.

The broken column above his grave signifies that he was the last male to bear the family name. Jean Balossy was clearly a very gallant young man, having been awarded the Legion d'Honneur and the Croix de Guerre. The cemetery is typical of many communal cemeteries in the area where sadly the graves of French soldiers killed in the conflict are often in a poor state; contrasting starkly with the well tended CWGC plots and the French national cemeteries.

Leave the cemetery and continue to Sancy-les-Cheminots and park by the church. The village was completely destroyed during the Great War and was reconstructed largely due to the efforts of Paul Busquet, the chief clerk of the regional railway and the president of the National Union of Railwaymen, Louis Olivier. With support from the American Committee for Devastated France, these men instigated the rebuilding of the village, despite the fact that it had already been decided by the authorities not to rebuild. Busquet's son, **Lucien**, died of his wounds in the German field lazarette which was located in the church during November 1914; he now rests with several others in the Garden of Remembrance which was opened in September 1925.

The grave of Lieutenant Jean Fernand Balossy at Celles-sur-Aisne.

The garden also hosts a memorial to **Quentin Roosevelt**, the aviator son of the US President, who was shot down and killed in July 1918

The Garden of Remembrance at
Sancy-les-Cheminots.

The memorial tablet to Theodore
Roosevelt at Sancy-les-Cheminots.

Theodore Roosevelt.

near Chamery. Roosevelt's remains are
now buried in the American Cemetery at
Colleville-sur-Mer.

In 1929 the village was renamed
Sancy-les-Cheminots in gratitude to the
railwaymen who contributed to the
rebuilding of the village. To find the
garden, walk uphill from the church and
continue over the road on the grassy track to the top of the hill.
Alternatively you can drive following the road past the church. The
garden is on your right. After returning to your vehicle, retrace your
route back to the D925 and turn left towards Vailly.

As you drive towards Vailly keep a sharp look-out for a turning on
the left to Vauxcelles Farm. Vauxcelles is where the Royal Scots were
billeted in the château after crossing the Aisne during the afternoon of
13 September, using the damaged Vailly Bridge. Drive slowly so you do
not miss the signpost to St. Pierre on the left, which is where the Royal
Irish were billeted on the same day. Shortly after the St. Pierre turning
you will come to Vailly British Cemetery **(10)** on the left. Park here.
The cemetery was made after the Armistice when graves were brought
in from other burial grounds and from the battlefields. The majority of
the 675 men buried here died in September 1914 and of these only 370
are identified. Here you will find **Captain Robert Frank Hawes**
(I.A.10.) of the 1/Leicesters, the first and only officer of the battalion

144

to be killed on the Aisne in 1914 and **Lieutenant Arthur Read** (IV.G.12.) of the Somersets. **Captain George Briggs** (III.A.2.) of the Royal Scots Fusiliers, who had seen service in South Africa and was mentioned in despatches for his work during the retreat from Mons, is in the top left hand corner. Also buried here

Captain Theodore Wright VC.

is **Captain Theodore Wright**, (II.B.21.) the Royal Engineer VC recipient, who won his cross at Mons and was killed on the Vailly bridge on 14 September, and **Major William Sarsfield** (II.C.11.), the acting commanding officer of the Connaught Rangers, who was killed on 20 September. William Sarsfield took over command of the battalion on 26 August after they had been

Captain Robert Frank Hawes. The only officer of 1/Leicesters to be killed on the Aisne.

severely dealt with at Le Grand Fayt during the retreat from Mons. He was commissioned into the battalion in 1888 and served all through the South African campaign. Other burials include **Lieutenant Herbert Hopkins** (I.A.8.), the medical officer attached to the Devonshire Regiment and **Brigadier General Neil Findlay** (VI.A.53.), the Chief Royal Artillery (CRA) officer to 1st Division. Findlay was the first British

Major William Sarsfield.

Brigadier General Neil Findlay.

officer of field rank to be killed in the Great War and, at 55-years-old, is the oldest casualty in the cemetery. **RSM Norman Macwhinnie** MC, DCM (I.H.29.) was one of the first 2/KOSB casualties of the battle and was killed near Sermoise on 13 September. 'There were 6 feet 5 inches of MacWhinnie, and every inch was good', wrote Robert Dolbey. The newly commissioned Second **Lieutenant Cosmo Gordon** (II.E.7.) of the Northamptons, who died of wounds received on the Chemin des Dames on 17 September, also rests here. Spare a moment to visit the youngest casualty, 16-year-old **Trumpeter Ivor James** (II.B.17.), who died of wounds. James was a former scholar at

145

Vailly British Cemetery.

the Duke of York's Military School at Dover and was serving with 128/Battery RFA when he was wounded and is very possibly the youngest British soldier to be killed in the 1914 campaign.

To the right is the extensive French National Cemetery, containing 1,576 burials. As with the British cemetery next door, this is a concentration cemetery where the remains of French soldiers from the surrounding area were brought in after the Armistice.

At the rear of the cemetery a marble obelisk commemorates *Sergent Felix Germain Jacouinot* and his comrades who were serving with the 120th Infantry Battalion. Felix Jacouinot was killed on 8 July 1917.

From the cemetery continue into Vailly taking the third turning on the left – Place Bouvines – and follow the road round to the right, passing the large car park on the left, to a crossroads. Go straight over and take the second turning on the right – Rue Saint-Precourd. Follow the

The French National Cemetery lies adjacent to the British cemetery at Vailly.

road round to the right and take the third turning on the right – Chemin de Rouge Maison. This minor road will take you up to Rouge Maison Farm **(11)**. As you approach the farm, the open ground on the left was approximately where **Gerard Kempthorne**, the 1/Lincolns medical officer, was captured. The British lines continued south of the farm to the east and clung to the edge of the high ground. Once at the farm, should you wish to stretch your legs a little, you can take a short walk towards La Fosse Marguet, a track which follows the approximate BEF line. Details of this and the walk to Folemprise Farm can be found in **Route 2 – La Rouge Maison Farm**, which also begins from here.

Leave the farm to drive north to meet the D15. Turn left at the T-junction and as you drive down towards Vailly, Rouge Maison farm is on your left. In Vailly, park near the church **(12)**. The original twelfth century church was almost completely destroyed by 1918 and was rebuilt on the original foundations. The old and new can clearly be seen as you walk round the building, some of which is pockmarked from shrapnel of Second World War vintage. The church and some of the surrounding buildings were used by 8/Field Ambulance as a dressing station and it was here that **Lieutenant Henry Robinson** worked with his colleagues dealing with the almost incessant flow of wounded. From the church the nightly convoys of ambulances would run the gauntlet crossing the river on the way to the casualty collection centres south of the river. After the British left for Flanders in October 1914, Vailly fell to the Germans in 1915.

Leave the church, follow the D14 to the river and the road bridge and park **(13)**. This is where the 3rd Division crossed the river on the damaged bridge after Lieutenant Cyril Martin of 56/Field Company found the canal bridge to be intact. Downstream of the road bridge is where the pontoon bridge was built by 56 and 57/Field Companies. This was also the scene of the death of **Captain Theodore Wright** VC of 57/Field Company whose grave you have just visited. The tour ends here.

CAR TOUR 2 – THE RIGHT FLANK

Start: The La Royère viewpoint
Finish: Paissy
Distance: 28 miles/48 kilometres

This tour takes the visitor into the right flank of the British sector. The tour begins at the La Royère viewpoint on the Chemin des Dames and after visiting Filain, travels to Braye-en-Laonnois, first visiting the quarries at Froidmont and thence down to Soupir. After a short excursion up to Soupir Farm and Chavonne we cross the river at Pont-Arcy and travel along the south bank to re-cross the river at Bourg-et Comin. The route then tracks the 1st Division attack up through Vendresse to Cerny-en-Laonnois. From Cerny we drive along the Chemin des Dames to the extreme right of the BEF line and thence to the end of the tour at Paissy.

The La Royère viewpoint (1) is 500 metres west of La Royère farm at the junction with the D152 on the Chemin des Dames. On reaching the junction turn into the observation point car park where there are numerous information panels and photographs describing the fighting

that took place on the Chemin des Dames and an interesting memorial to French colonial troops. From the observation platform it is possible to see for some considerable distance to the north across the Ailette valley and beyond. You will also be able to see the tiny chapel of St Berthe in the foreground, which is our next port of call. Turn right out of the car park continue down the D152 towards Filain for some 500 metres until you see the chapel on your right. Park here.

The chapel of St Berthe.

In 1814 the chapel was burnt by the Cossacks before being totally destroyed in the Great War. Rebuilt in 1932, the chapel was a regular destination for pilgrims for the next eight years, particularly as the nearby spring reputedly cured fevers and ailments. Today it is suffering sadly from neglect as are the commemorative plaques to French units involved in the 1917 fighting on the outside walls.

Continue to Filain and park near the church (2). The village was in

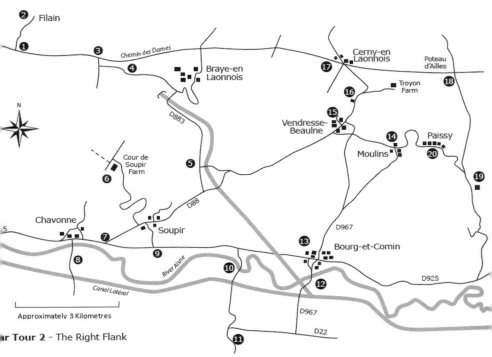

German hands from the night of 12 September 1914, when it was occupied by the German *2nd Cavalry Division* who were pushed into the gap in the German line and which was still a source of concern to OHL. It was also the location of a large German field lazarette.

In the small communal churchyard cemetery next to the church you will find the graves of three British soldiers who died in September 1914. **Private E Tyas** of the Lincolnshire Regiment was killed on 20 September, while **Private H Brown** of the Royal Scots Fusiliers died on 22 September along with **Private Herbert Chitty** of the Royal Fusiliers. Given the location of their graves it is probable that these men died of their wounds after being captured on the high ground above Vailly in the Rouge

The churchyard cemetery at Filain.

Maison Farm area on 14 September. **Gerard Kempthorne**, the 1/Lincolns medical officer, was brought here after his capture along with several other wounded British casualties. Before you leave see if you can spot the German memorial in the churchyard, it is now in a very poor condition but is dedicated to the dead of both sides.

149

Leave the village and return to the D18, turning left along the Chemin des Dames. Drive slowly as you will pass four memorials on the right side of the road. The first is dedicated to 99th Regiment of Artillery, which fought here in 1917 and in June 1940 and a little further along the road is the memorial to the 19-year-old **Jean Robin**, who died fighting with the 146th Regiment of Infantry. Bear in mind this is not a good place to stop as there are no lay-bys along this section of the Chemin des Dames. The next two memorials are closely associated with the wooded area you can see on the left of the road.

The first memorial remembers 20-year-old **Jean Dauly** and the second is dedicated to 20-year-old **Marcel Duquenoy**. Both men were serving with the 350th Regiment of Infantry on 6 May 1917 and were killed in the wooded area on the left. Very often a French national flag can be seen draped on the fringes of the wood, along with a white cross of remembrance.

Take the next turning on the right **(3)** signposted Braye-en-Laonnais and Ostel and shortly afterwards take the next left turning towards Braye. In approximately one hundred and twenty five metres you should be able to see a track heading up into the wooded area on the left. Park off the road and walk up the track, which once led to Froidmont Farm, to find the entrance to the Froidmont quarries **(4)** and the memorial to the American 26th Infantry Division.

The entrance to the Froidmont quarries and the memorial to the American 26th Division.

Sadly the quarries are now closed to the public but they were occupied by the Americans in early 1918 and the French 101st and 102nd Infantry. From the base of the flagpole look left for views of Braye. As you walk back to your vehicle notice that the ground on the right is pockmarked with shell holes.

Continue into Braye, bearing right at the war memorial, to cross the bridge over the canal. As you cross the bridge glance right to see the tunnel entrance, which takes the canal under the Chemin des Dames ridge. Braye is no stranger to conflict. Part of the village was burned by the Russian forces in March 1814, forcing the inhabitants to seek shelter in the quarries, while in 1914 it was fortified by the Germans. Prior to the Nivelle offensive in 1917 the village was destroyed by French shellfire but it was not until October 1917 that the French finally occupied the ruined village. A short re-occupation by the Germans in May 1918 concluded with its final liberation by Italian troops in October 1918.

After crossing the bridge bear left down the valley. Above, and high up on the right, you will be able to see the white stonework of the monument dedicated to the *27th* and *67th Battalions de Chasseurs Alpins* (mountain infantry) who fought here in 1917. You are now in the valley up which 6 Brigade attacked on the morning of 14 September 1914.

Continue down the valley alongside the canal until you reach Lock Number 11, which is located just north of the D88 road bridge. Pull into the open space by the lock and park. As you walk towards the old lock keeper's house, the former site of La Metz Farm **(5)** is on the left amongst the trees. This is where the 1/Berkshires had their battalion HQ in September 1914. A close inspection will reveal the old moat which once surrounded the farm buildings. If you look back up the

The site of la Metz farm in the Braye valley.

valley you can see the line of the Chemin des Dames ridge, which was the brigade objective for 14 September.

After leaving the lock do not cross the canal but continue straight ahead to the junction with the D88. Turn right towards Soupir. Just before you enter the village look across to the left to see the Soupir arch, all that is left of the once grand château that stood in these grounds. Once in Soupir, park near the church. There are two cemeteries containing BEF graves in the village; the first is directly behind the church and was the burial ground used by the field

The Soupir arch.

Soupir church and cemetery.

ambulance units based at the Cour de Soupir Farm and Soupir Château. Initially 3/ Cavalry Field Ambulance were based at the château but on 17 September 4/Field Ambulance took it over. The ruined château was not finally demolished until 1930. In Soupir Churchyard Cemetery there are thirty 1914 burials, including the three Ox and Bucks officer casualties from the quarry disaster at Cour de Soupir on 16 September. These include the Berkshire cricketer, **Lieutenant Hugh Mockler-Ferryman**, 18-year-old **Second Lieutenant Paul Girardot**, who had only been commissioned since February 1914, and **Lieutenant Reginald Worthington**, who was awarded the Croix de Chevalier of the Legion d'Honnneur. **Gunners H Fuller** and **J Smith**, who were serving with 1/Siege Battery (not 39/Siege Battery, as recorded by the CWGC) are also buried here, victims of a premature explosion. The battery were using the obsolete 6-inch guns at the time and firing extremely old and rather unstable ammunition. The rebuilt church still bears the scars from the Second World War. Soupir Communal Cemetery is only a short walk away and can be found by taking the road directly opposite the church – Rue de Paris – and turning right up a steep minor road.

The CWGC corner of the cemetery is very much a Guards Brigade enclave and many of the casualties from the fighting around Cour de Soupir Farm on 14 and 15 September are buried here. Made up largely of officers, the cemetery contains sixteen named burials, all brought in

Soupir Communal Cemetery.

Captain Lord Arthur Hay.

Captain Lord Guernsey.

after the Armistice from their original burial grounds. **Major Arthur Green**, Brigade Major of 17 Brigade, is the only officer who was not fighting with 4 Guards Brigade. 40-year-old Arthur Green had been awarded the DSO in South Africa and arrived on the Aisne with the 6th Division on 19 September. Notable Guards casualties include: **Captains Lord Arthur Hay, Lord Guernsey, Hon William Cecil** and **Lieutenants Frederick Des Voeux** and **Richard Welby.** Second Lieutenant **Richard Lockwood** from Romford was killed with the 2/Coldstream and 19-year-old **John Pickersgill-Cuncliffe** was the Grenadier officer who was shot dead whilst lying wounded on the battlefield.

Retrace your steps to the church and your vehicle. You are now looking for the D1900 to take you up to La Cour de Soupir Farm **(6)**. The

Captain Lord Guernsey.

road is steep in places and has a number of sharp bends; as you approach the south eastern corner of the farm slow down and glance over to the densely vegetated slope on the right. Amongst this tangle of vegetation is what remains of the quarry that was hit by a German shell on 16 September, killing and wounding over one hundred men of the Guards and Ox and Bucks Light Infantry. Continue uphill, bearing left until you reach a T-junction. To the left is the farm and the farm track that eventually leads down to Chavonne. We are turning right along the minor road to a point where there is an obvious large tree and a pylon.

There is plenty of parking here. This is the high ground of the Croix sans Tête where **Major Sarsfield**, commanding the Connaught Rangers, positioned his outposts early on 14 September. As you look back

154

The German view of Cour de Soupir farm.

towards the farm, which is almost due south from where you are standing, you get the view the attacking Germans would have had that morning as they approached the farm. Looking left to right, the wooded area is the Bois de la Bovette where the Irish and Coldstream Guards lost so heavily to German snipers on 14 September. The woods fall steeply down to the Braye valley. It was in these woods that the Guard's finally got in contact with the 1/KRRC, who were on the left flank of 6 Brigade. On the right is La Cour de Soupir Farm, which was the focus of the German attacks and further to the right are the wooded slopes above Chavonne.

Return to the T-junction and continue downhill to Soupir. As the road twists and turns you can get a good view of the lake that was once a feature of Soupir Château gardens. Turn right in Soupir and continue along the D88 until you reach the Italian cemetery **(7)** on the right. Park here. The 593 men buried here are largely from the Italian II Corps, which fought in the area during September and October 1918, taking Soupir from the Germans on 1 October. At the rear of the cemetery is a striking Fernand Cian sculpture, which was erected in 1921 in memory of all Italian soldiers who fell in the Great War.

After leaving the cemetery continue to Chavonne and take the first turning on the left to cross the bridge on the D884

The Fernand Cian sculpture in the Italian cemetery.

155

Chavonne, the view from south of the river.

towards Cys-la-Commune. After 200 metres or so stop **(8)** and look back towards the village.

This is the view the 4 Guards Brigade had on 13 September as they began approaching the river. To the left of the bridge is the high ground of Les Grinons where Number 2 Company of 2/Coldstream Guards was left on the night of 13 September after **Brigadier General Fielding**

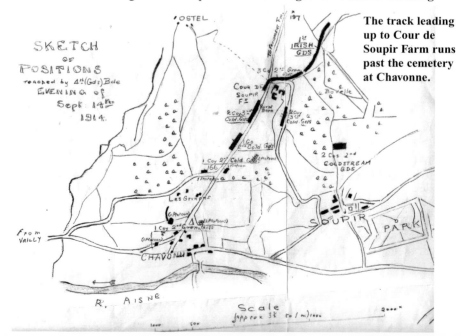

The track leading up to Cour de Soupir Farm runs past the cemetery at Chavonne.

ordered the remainder of the brigade back across the river to Cys-la-Commune for the night.

To the right of the bridge and above the large house is the communal cemetery. Hidden from view is the minor road that runs past the cemetery and soon degrades into a steep track rising steeply through the woods towards La Cour de Soupir Farm. As **Major Lord Bernard Gordon Lennox** remarked in his diary, it is fortunate that the commanding heights above the village were not strongly held.

Turn your vehicle round and re-cross the river, turning right onto the D925. Continue past the junction with the D88 until you reach Soupir French National Cemetery No1 **(9)** on your left and park.

Here both German and French dead lie alongside each other. There is no physical barrier between the two plots, just a change from the black German headstones to the white French crosses. In the German plot there are 11,179 burials of which 5,184 have headstones. Most headstones bear the names of at least two, and sometimes more, names on each face of the headstone. A further 5,995 are buried in the mass grave in the centre of the plot and of these only 794 are identified, their names inscribed on the panels seen at ground level. The French

Soupir French National Cemetery No1 with the German cemetery in the foreground.

cemetery was initially begun as the burial ground associated with a nearby casualty clearing station; enlarged in 1920 it now contains 7,806 French soldiers, one Russian and one Belgian. Half of the burials have their own marked headstone but there are three mass graves holding the remains of some 3,088 fallen Frenchmen. In 1934 Soupir No 2 was opened across the road and now contains 2,829 soldiers and civilians killed in the two world wars. On the extreme left and towards the rear of the cemetery are two CWGC headstones, marking the last resting place of unknown British soldiers. This is a remarkably poignant place and a stark reminder of the tragic cost of war that dominated the first half of the twentieth century in Europe.

After leaving the cemeteries drive slowly so as not to miss the first of two gates on the left that once led to Soupir Château.

The rusting gates that once led to Soupir Château.

Some 800 metres further on is the second set of gates and beyond them, running down the side of the quarry workings, are the remains of part of the old château wall. Drive on until you reach the turning on the right to Pont-Arcy. Before you turn onto the D228 cast a glance ahead to see the old Pont-Arcy railway station on the right, now a private house. Follow the D228 over the bridge **(10)** and stop where convenient.

This is the bridge that was repaired by 11/Field Company while

The modern road bridge at Pont-Arcy.

5/Field Company constructed a pontoon bridge upstream of the road bridge. One of the first battalions to cross the river at Pont-Arcy on 13 September was the 2/Connaught Rangers who, under fire, used the partly submerged single girder that remained of the road bridge and took up positions on the north bank where they remained covering the crossing by the remainder of 5 Brigade over the pontoon bridge.

Drive on over the Canal Latéral towards Veil-Arcy, following the road round to the right through the village to the communal cemetery **(11)** on the D22. There is only one BEF burial here, that of **Lieutenant Colonel Charles Dalton**, the RAMC officer who was wounded at Verneuil Château on 19 September and died of his wounds in the nearby CCS. Turn your vehicle round, and before you continue, look to the north for good views of the Chemin des Dames on the skyline and to the right you should be able to see Bourg-et-Comin.

At the next junction turn right along the D22 and take the second turning on the left to Bourg-et-Comin. The first two bridges **(12)** you cross were taken by 4/Royal Irish Dragoon Guards on the morning of 13 September and it was on the first bridge across the Canal Latéral that the cavalrymen took their casualties.

The second canal bridge was soon in the hands of the dragoons but the road bridge was impassable, having been destroyed by the German rearguard. It was from the second bridge that the towpath along the canal was accessed using the aqueduct.

As you cross the second canal bridge slow down and glance across to the left for a view of the aqueduct. Constructed in the late nineteenth century, the thirty one mile long canal passes over the river using the aqueduct before it continues under the Chemin des Dames at Braye on its way to Abbécourt. The infrastructure of the canal, including the aqueduct and tunnel section, was completely destroyed during the war and re-constructed after the armistice. As far as the BEF was concerned the aqueduct was rendered useless on 21 September when it was wrecked by a shell but by that time alternative bridging points were in place. The aqueduct can be visited by walking along the towpath from the road bridge situated a kilometre west of Bourg on the D925.

After crossing the river continue into Bourg, take the second turning on the left and park in the car park near the church. Walk up the Rue de la Boise to the cemetery **(13)**. There are eleven identified burials here of 1914 vintage

The canal bridge at Bourg.

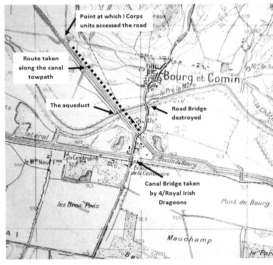

Cameron Highlanders at Bourg Communal Cemetery.

and, with the exception of **Pioneer Richard Arthur** of 1/Signal Company, the result of two separate incidents.

The 4/Dragoon Guards casualties are all from 13 September when the regiment took the bridges you have just crossed. **Captain Gerald 'Pat' Fitzgerald** had only been married to Dorothy Charrington for just

159

Captain Gerald Fitzgerald.

over five weeks when he was shot through the head by a sniper in the church tower. Also buried here are **Lance Corporal William Baker**, 27-year-old **Corporal Francis Chapman** and **Private Harry Savory**, all serving with the 4/Dragoon Guards.

Harry Savory was a settler in Rhodesia in 1896 and served through the whole of the Matebele War. In South Africa he won a DCM before serving at a lieutenant in the Imperial Light Horse. On the outbreak of war he enlisted in the Irish Dragoon Guards as a private soldier. Six of the Cameron Highlanders from the cave disaster of 25 September are also here. **Captain Douglas Miers**, who was commanding the battalion at the time, was killed on the same day and month as his brother, Captain Ronald Miers, had been killed in South Africa in 1901. **Captain Napier Cameron** served in the Scottish Horse in South Africa and joined the battalion in 1908. His daughter Honor was born in December 1914, ten weeks after his death. **Captain Allan Cameron** also fought in South Africa and was adjutant of the 1/Lovat Scouts until 1911, when he re-joined his battalion and then left with them for France. Although not technically a Cameron Highlander, **Lieutenant John Crocket** was the medical officer attached to the battalion. Crocket qualified at Edinburgh University and joined the RAMC in 1913 and was tending wounded when the cave collapsed. The remaining two Cameron Highlanders are **Private Robert Brown** and 35-year-old **RSM George Burt** DCM.

Return to your vehicle and leave the car park to rejoin the D967. Turn left at the roundabout, continuing on the D967 to Moulins. Just before you enter the village you will see La Tuilerie Farm on your right. It was here on 24 September that 2/Siege Battery with its obsolete 6-inch Howitzers, under the command of **Major G S MacKenzie**, was in position amongst the trees to the right of the modern day D 967 just southwest of the farm.

The forward observation post was on the high ground of Mont de Charmont, some 150 metres across to the left. 22-year-old **Gunner Thomas Lacey** died here as the result of a premature explosion. Once in Moulins keep bearing left to join the D1840 to find the communal

Moulins Communal Cemetery.

Lieutenant Colonel Adrian Grant Duff and Lieutenant William Polson.

Captain Douglas Lucas-Tooth.

cemetery **(14)** on the right. Park here and walk up to the entrance. Alternatively you can park by the church in the village centre and walk.

The ten burials here include **Lieutenant Colonel Adrian Grant Duff**, the Black Watch commanding officer who was killed on 14 September and **Lieutenant William Polson**, killed by the same shell. **Captain Douglas Lucas-Tooth** of 9/Lancers was another victim of shellfire. Tragically all three sons of Sir Robert Lucas-Tooth died in the Great War; Selwyn, a captain in the Lancashire Fusiliers, on 20 October 1914 and Leonard, a major in the Honourable Artillery Company, in July 1918. After Leonard's death the baronetcy became extinct. The Scottish rugby union international, **Lieutenant Ronald Simpson**, who was killed on 15 September with 16/Battery RFA, is also buried here. Simpson was the first rugby international – of any nationality – to die in the war. Four soldiers of the 1/Queen's rest here, including 19-year-old **Private Archibald Shapley** from London, who most probably died of his wounds on 19 September in the 1/Field Ambulance dressing station that was situated in the village.

Lieutenant Ronald Simpson.

After leaving the cemetery continue along the D1840 towards Vendresse-Beaulne. Turn right at the T-junction and take the minor road into the village centre and park by the Mairie. The cemetery **(15)** is at

161

the rear of the church and the CWGC plot is in the right hand corner. This is a surprisingly large concentration of burials given the size of the churchyard and there are now over eighty casualties commemorated here.

Of these, half are unidentified and special memorials commemorate thirty five soldiers known to be buried here among them. Amongst the more notable are **Captain Riversdale 'Rivy' Grenfell** of the 9/Lancers and **Major James Johnston**, who commanded 115/Battery RFA. Johnston fought in South Africa, was mentioned in despatches twice and receiving a brevet majority in 1902. **Major John Carpenter-Garnier** of the 1/Scots Guards was hit by shrapnel on 14 September.

This South African veteran died of wounds the next day and was one of four officers of the battalion killed on the Aisne. Another South African veteran is **Captain Harold Casamajor Davies**, who was killed on 26 September. He joined the Welsh Regiment as a second lieutenant in 1900 and died serving with the 2nd Battalion. Outside of the main plot is 22-year-old **Second Lieutenant John Manley**, a special reserve officer serving with 26/Field Company. He was killed by shellfire on

26 September whilst he, and No 4 Section, were maintaining the line near the Sucrerie. The former Cheltenham scholar was brought down to the churchyard later that night and buried by the men of his section. What is also particularly noticeable is the poor state of many of the

The entrance to Vendresse Communal Cemetery.
The CWGC plot at Vendresse Communal Cemetery.

headstones marking the graves of French soldiers. Before you leave the village take a short walk up the road heading northwest towards the woods at the back of the churchyard. This is probably one of the tracks taken by **Lieutenant Colonel John Ponsonby** and the 1/Coldstream Guards on the morning of 14 September as they moved up towards the Sucrerie at the Cerny crossroads.

From Vendresse return to the D967 and turn left to reach Vendresse British Cemetery **(16)** which is signposted. This is a concentration cemetery containing casualties from both 1914 and 1918. There are over 700 British burials here, over half of which are unidentified and, of these, 245 are from 1914. Here you will find **Lieutenant Thomas Meautys** (III.J.10.), who was killed on 20 September during the attack on the West Yorkshire trenches. Thomas Meautys had only been married for a little over two months before he sailed for France with the 6th Division. He was never to see his son Thomas, who was born in April 1915. A further eight casualties from the attacks of 20 September are buried here, including **Major Alexander Robb** (I.K.5.) of the 2/Durham Light Infantry who – like Sir Douglas Haig before him – was a recipient of the Anson Memorial Sword at Sandhurst. Twice mentioned in despatches on the Northwest Frontier in 1898, this distinguished

The entrance to Vendresse British Cemetery.

officer died of his wounds. **Lieutenant John O'Connell** (I.E.10.) was the RAMC doctor attached to the Highland Light Infantry. Another casualty killed in the Cameron Highlanders' cave disaster of 25 September was **Lieutenant Kenneth Meiklejohn** (III.C.4.), the Cameron Highlander's adjutant, who was died eleven days after the Royal Sussex adjutant, **Lieutenant Hon Herbert Pelham**, the son of the Earl of Chichester (I.C.15). Pelham died on 14 September, alongside **Lieutenant Colonel Ernest Montresor**, on the Chemin des Dames. Also here is the nephew of novelist Rider Haggard, **Captain Mark Haggard** (I.G.11), who was carried to safety by VC winner Lance Corporal William Fuller of 2/Welsh. **Captain Dugald Gilkison**, (III.C.6), serving with the Cameronians, was another casualty of 20 September. His brother James, a lieutenant with the Argyll and Sutherland Highlanders, was killed at Le Cateau on 26 August 1914. Overall, some ninety three of the identified individuals who are buried here fell on either 14 or 15 September, a number which included 23-

year-old **Private Frank Read** (IV.G.2.) of the 1/Coldstream Guards, from Quainton in Buckinghamshire. Read was one of John Ponsonby's men and would have probably have been killed near the Sucrerie.

Return to the D967 and continue uphill for 150 metres and take the unmarked minor road on the right to Troyon Farm. The hamlet of Troyon, which was noted by **Lieutenant Jack Needham** from the Northampton lines on the Chemin des Dames, was not rebuilt after the war and all that remains today is the farm and the walled cemetery, which is now empty apart from three obvious graves. It was here that the 2/Sherwood Foresters were resting when the call came on 20 September to retake the trenches on the Chemin des Dames that had been abandoned by the West Yorkshires. With the farmhouse on your left, look across the valley to the steep eastern side; this was where the Foresters would have climbed up to reach the Yorkshires' trenches on the Chemin des Dames.

Return to the D967 and turn right, following the road as it bends round to the left. Slow down here as you will quickly come to a track that cuts across the road in front of you. It was on this line that the German outposts were positioned on the morning of 14 September when they were disturbed by the 9/Lancers. Drive on to the Cerny

The position of the Sucrerie at Cerny crossroads depicted on a 1917 French trench map.

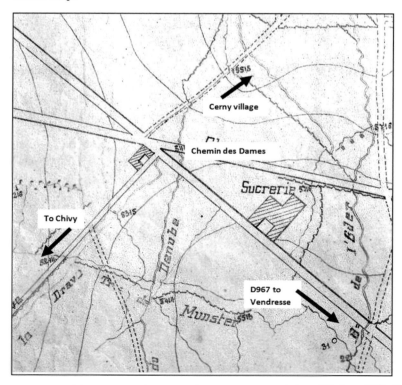

crossroads, **(17)** passing the former site of the Sucrerie on your right, and park behind the chapel.

The memorial chapel and the lantern to the dead were not erected until 1950 and today are maintained by the volunteers of the Chemin des Dames Memorial Committee, who are responsible for the annual ceremony held on the anniversary of the Nivelle offensive.

Outside the chapel there are information boards giving a brief history of the fighting that took place here; while inside the chapel walls are covered with memorial plaques, including one unveiled by the Senegalese president in 1980 in memory of the Senegalese killed on the Chemin des Dames in 1917. In the right hand corner is a small statue of Saint Remigius, who became Bishop of Reims in 460, a position he held until his death in 533. Between the wars a wooden cafe building stood on this site, staffed by veterans of the Great War.

Across the road the French cemetery was created between 1919 and 1925 and contains the graves of over 5,000 French soldiers and fifty-four Russian soldiers who

The memorial chapel at Cerny.

The interior of the memorial chapel, a permanent reminder of the French sacrifice on the Chemin des Dames.

The cafe-restaurant that once stood on the site of the memorial chapel.

The German and French cemeteries at the Cerny crossroads.

The German dead are often buried two or more to a grave.

fought with the French in 1917. Sadly some 2,300 remain unidentified and are buried together in a mass grave.

The German cemetery is accessed at the rear of the French plot and originally contained the graves of over 5,000 German soldiers. In 1924 it was enlarged to accommodate burials that were brought in from the surrounding area. Today there are some 7,500 graves and, as with the French cemetery, it contains a mass grave at the rear of the plot where nearly 4,000 unidentified soldiers were buried together. Interestingly, there are twelve graves of Jewish soldiers something that the visitor to the Malmaison German Second World War cemetery will not find amongst the headstones. The cemetery was also the symbolic venue of a meeting between Chancellor Adenauer and General de Gaulle on 8 July 1962 prior to the Franco-German treaty of 1963.

Leave the cemetery and walk along to the crossroads. To your right is the tall column of the

The memorial to the 1st Battalion Loyal North Lancashire Regiment.

memorial to the 1/Loyal North Lancs, enclosed by iron railings and now without its screen of evergreens.

From the memorial walk down the D967 back towards Vendresse; on the left are a collection of private dwellings and it was on this plot of land that the Sucrerie stood in 1914. If you walk a little further on you may still find one of the last remnants of it in the form of a blue and white sign still clinging to a post near to what may have been an entrance to the now long gone building. From here as you look down the road towards Vendresse you will get the German view of the battlefield on the morning of 14 September. As the German outposts were driven in by the 2/KRRC, the German soldiers at the Sucrerie would have seen the British fanning out left and right as they topped the rise.

One of the last vestiges of the old Cerny Sucrerie.

The German view from the Sucrerie as the advancing British spread out at the top of the high ground.

Across to the right the first signs of the Coldstream Guards and the Cameron Highlanders would have been evident as they approached the Sucrerie.

Walk back towards your vehicle, keeping the memorial chapel on your left and stop at the Mairie building. Outside the building is another memorial, *aux enfants de Cerny-en-Laonnois*.

At the Cerny crossroads continue straight on along the Chemin des Dames. Along this road for the next one and a half miles were the only

British trench lines that occupied the Chemin des Dames ridge. It was along here and to the left of the road that the infamous white flag incident of 17 September took place involving the Northamptons, the KRRC and the Queen's. Just after you pass the monument to the 24-years-old **Sous-Lieutenant Louis Astoul**, a track leads off to the left. This was the line of the 1/Queen's advance on 14 September when they crossed the Chemin des Dames on their way to take La Bovelle Farm.

The farm was not rebuilt after the war but was the scene of some costly close quarter fighting after the Queen's were surrounded. Apart from John Ponsonby's tiny mixed force at Cerny, the advance made by the Queen's was the furthest made by any battalion during the whole campaign. At around 2pm the battalion retired to the Chemin des Dames.

Drive on to the obvious crossroads at Poteau d'Ailles Farm and park **(18)**. You are now at the highest point of the Chemin des Dames ridge at 199 metres.

The Queen's war diary tells us this crossroads was the furthest point of the British line on the right and was the point where it linked up with the French Fifth Army. The Queen's held this section of the line, with the Northamptons on their left, until 18 September, after which they were relieved by the Coldstream Guards. On the day before their relief they lost both their commanding officer and adjutant, who were both killed by sniper fire. The road heading north past the farm once led to the village of Ailles, another of the lost villages of the Aisne. Occupied by the Germans in September 1914 and emptied of its inhabitants, the village was destroyed by French shellfire in April 1917. Today, just under a mile down this road, all that remains is the Ailles Memorial,

which was erected in 1932 by the Touring Club de France.

At the crossroads take the D102 towards Paissy. Ignore the turning for Paissy on your right and continue for another 500 yards to La Tour de Paissy Farm **(19)**, which you will see on the left.

The farm occupied a high point from which it was possible to view the whole of the line along the Chemin des Dames. On the morning of 20

Tour de Paissy Farm.

September, the telescope, which was used to survey the line, was not working and the staff officers at the farm failed to realize the advancing lines of infantry were in fact Germans! From the farm you can see the Poteau d'Ailles crossroads clearly.

Turn your vehicle round and take the D888 on the left to Paissy village **(20)**. Find a suitable parking place near the church, which is situated at the far end of the village on the high ground above the road. A walk along the one main street – Rue Principale – is highly recommended as each house has access to its own cave, many of which have been converted into more permanent structures. Across on the other side of the bowl of the valley you can see numerous large caves.

It was in the village caves that British soldiers and the local inhabitants sheltered from German shellfire. Arthur Osburn, the medical officer serving with the 4/Royal Irish Dragoon Guards, recorded how he used the caves to treat injured French soldiers. Just before the Rue de l'Eglise you will find the Mairie and a number of information boards.

Walk on up to the church to visit the CWGC plot in the churchyard.

Near the entrance is an information board about the Paissy caves and

Caves at Paissy village.

Paissy church and communal cemetery.

**Lieutenant Colonel
Dawson Warren.**

their history. Go through the churchyard gate and walk round to the left, where you will find the CWGC headstones. There are five BEF soldiers here including **Captain Augustus Cathcart**, who was killed at Cerny on 14 September serving as a company commander with 2/KRRC. **Lieutenant Colonel Dawson Warren** and his adjutant, **Captain Charles Wilson** of the 1/Queen's are both buried here after being killed by sniper fire on 17 September.

Dawson Warren joined the Queen's in 1885 as a lieutenant and after a distinguished career was appointed to command his battalion in March 1913. Charles Wilson was appointed adjutant in October 1913 and was awarded the Legion d'Honneur shortly after his death. Also buried here is **Gunner Thomas Connor** from 135 Battery and **Private Conrad Kenward** of 2/Royal Sussex. Kenward enlisted in January 1911 at Chichester and died of wounds on 21 September and most probably took part in the counter attack on the West Yorkshires' trenches the previous day. The tour finishes here.

WALKING AND BIKING THE BATTLEFIELD

The Aisne valley is fortunate that the *Grande Randonée* 12 (GR12) traverses the northern slopes of the valley for some fifty kilometres, taking in much of the British sector as it meanders across the landscape. For the tourist who wishes to combine a walking or biking holiday with battlefield history, this long distance path, which runs from Amsterdam to Paris, is the ideal way of exploring the area. In France there is no footpath/bridleway distinction, French land access is governed by the simple rule that you can go anywhere you like as long as you act responsibly and no-one tells you not to. However, private land owners have the right to ban you from their land and the local Mayor can also pass an *arreté municipal*, which may ban particular user-groups from a given trail. That said, not everyone has the time or indeed the energy for such a long distance enterprise and, to that end, the four local routes, each of which are personally known to the author, should provide a more intimate access to the front line and allow the visitor to explore some of the more remote parts of this fascinating battlefield. As with the car tours, the numbers in the text **(1)** relate to the numbers found on the maps. Each route has been superimposed on the 1:20,000 1918 map of the area and you should be aware that some of the marked tracks on it no longer exist today.

ROUTE 1 – LA MONTAGNE FARM

Suitable for: 🚲 🚶

Distance: 3.2 miles/5.12 km
Grade: Moderate with two steep sections

This circular route begins at Bucy-le-Long in the square by the Mairie, which is on the Rue Géneral de Gaulle. We follow the path that **Lieutenant Gerald Whittuck** and the Somerset Light Infantry probably took as they climbed above the village in the early hours of 13 September to occupy the high ground to the left of the Hampshires. The route continues along the edge of the high ground, past La Montagne Farm, to visit the Rifle Brigade positions above Le Moncel. Apart from the off-road sections the route is on a good surface and within the capabilities of most battlefield tourists.

From the car park **(1)** walk north along the Rue Georges Clemenceau to reach the Rue Chemin des Dames. Turn left here and follow the road as it bears round to the left and begins to rise gently uphill. Should you wish to visit the church, turn left along the Rue Felix Bruin. The church was used by 10/Field Ambulance as a forward dressing station and completely destroyed during the Great War, as was the whole village.

The re-built church was an almost exact replica of the original. From

the church retrace your steps and continue uphill on the D95 along the Rue Chemin des Dames, passing the gates of a château on the left. Look carefully at the right hand pillar to see evidence of what appears to be 1914 graffiti.

Just after the last house on the left and before you reach the communal cemetery, look across to your left for fine views of Soissons Cathedral. Ahead of you is Bucy-le-Long Communal Cemetery **(2)**. There are two separate plots here. The plot containing the CWGC graves is directly in front of you with the green CWGC sign on the left of

The church at Bucy-le-Long. The château gates on the Rue Chemin des Dames.

1914 graffiti on the gate posts.

the entrance gate. The two 1914 burials are towards the rear of the cemetery on the right.

Riflemen Sydney Cridland and **Albert Hammond** were both serving with the 1st Rifle Brigade and killed quite late on in the campaign when the Rifle Brigade were in the line north of La Montagne Farm. Close by is an imposing statue of a 22-year-old French soldier, **Paul Brodin**, who was killed in action on 1 January 1915, another touching reminder of the extensive French involvement on this front.

Leave the cemetery by the top gate and turn left uphill. The road is used by local traffic, so where possible it is sensible to walk on the pathway inside the road barrier on the left. Turn into the woods at the next obvious turning on the left **(3)** crossing over the small stream issuing from the 'source' on the right. Continue straight ahead of you up the steep track which rises for approximately 250 metres before a narrow path on the right leads directly up to a large cave entrance. This

The headstones of Riflemen Sydney Cridland and Albert Hammond.

Regimental carvings in the limestone of the cave above Bucy-le-Long.
The Hampshire regimental crest carved by Sergeant Frederick Brisley in 1914.

Sergeant Frederick Brisley.

entrance is easy to miss, particularly in the summer months when the vegetation is quite dense. The cave was a short distance from the front line. Amongst the numerous regimental badges carved into the limestone, which can be viewed without entering the cave, you will find that of the Hampshire Regiment, carved by **Sergeant Frederick Brisley**. He was later commissioned into the Royal West Surrey Regiment and survived the war.

Retrace your steps carefully to the road and turn left. Almost directly across the road on the right another track leads steeply up through the woods. Cross the road and take this track which will bring you out at the edge of the open ground of the spur **(4)**. You are now standing on the approximate British line which ran north of the cave you have just visited, across the fields to the east to the 1/Rifle Brigade positions above Le Moncel. La Montagne Farm **(5)** is visible some 450 metres to the south. To reach the farm, continue along the road and bear left round the bend in the road. Completely destroyed during the war, the farm was rebuilt almost exactly on its original site. It was here that 31 and 55/Howitzer Batteries were in place providing support to the French advance north of Soissons across to the west. From this point are good views up towards the crest of the spur on the left and across to the right. Looking towards the river it is still possible to see across to Vénizel bridge and the flat water meadows over which the 4th Division battalions advanced on 12/13 September. On a clear day it is also possible to see the curve in the D95 where the road was diverted after the war to cross the modern day river bridge. Binoculars are useful here.

The road you are standing on eventually becomes an unmetaled track heading northeast. In just over 800 metres you will come to a junction of tracks. Stop just before the junction and turn to look back along the track. You are now in the sector of the line occupied by the 1/Rifle Brigade on 13 September. To your right were the Rifle Brigade reserve trenches, where two companies would have been positioned. Now continue to the junction **(6)**. Straight ahead along the edge of the track heading away from you would have been a further company position. Just north of the bend in the track the large depression in the ground was occupied by one company in a trench system with a

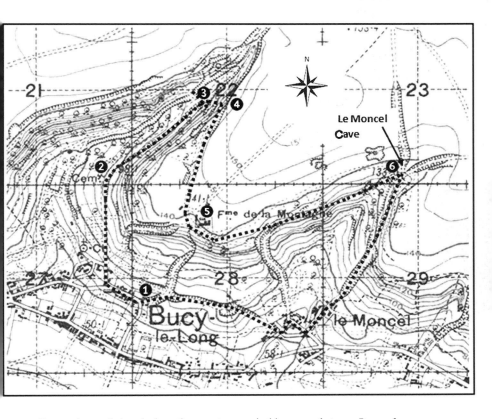

forward trench just below the crest occupied by one platoon. It was here that **Lieutenant Cecil Brereton** and the guns of 68/Battery were in action and from where the Rifle Brigade made their initial advance to the crest of the spur on 13 September. The German lines were a little over 600 metres to the north. Now find the short path leading through a cutting which will take you to the entrance to Le Moncel Cave.

According to the Rifle Brigade war diary, the cave was home to battalion HQ, a large number of horses and men, together with the battalion transport. The cave also provided shelter from shellfire.

Retrace your steps and turn left downhill, this was probably the route used by the battalions holding this part of the line as they moved to and from the front line and the route taken by Cecil Brereton and 68/Battery. Bear right at the next junction to the outskirts of Bucy-le-Long. This is the Rue de Moncel. At the T-junction with Rue Victor Hugo turn right to another T-junction and turn left into Rue de Château. Take the next right into Rue de Montail and at the next T-junction turn left and continue along the road which eventually becomes a track across open ground. The track will bring you to a small crossroads, go straight ahead and follow the Rue Besseville back to the car park.

Le Moncel Cave.

ROUTE 2 – ROUGE MAISON FARM

Suitable for: 🚲 🎏

Distance: 3.8 miles/6.12 km

Grade: Moderate

The British front line above Vailly is difficult to pinpoint accurately. The maps drawn at the time and found in battalion war diaries can be a little confusing and somewhat lacking in detail and scale. However, the map drawn by Lieutenant Billy Congreve does give a reasonable impression of the line above Vailly. From his map, and the war diaries of the battalions who served in this sector, we know that the front line was south of La Rouge Maison Farm and ran from Vauxelles in the west, across the Pièce de la Justice, and skirted the head of the valley south of the farm before heading towards La Fosse Marguet. The Ostel road was the approximate eastern boundary of the salient. Our route begins at Rouge Maison Farm and visits Folemprise Farm and the former site of Rochefort Farm, before it follows the eastern edge of the spur to the Verne family monument – which was the approximate line taken by the Germans on 20 September, when they broke through the British line

Drive up to the farm and park at the crossroads **(1)** amongst the farm

The track from Rouge Maison farm looking towards Folemprise farm.

Folemprise Farm

Chemin des Dames

Rouge Maison Farm

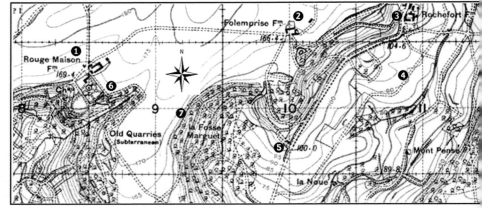

buildings. The farm remained in German hands during the British campaign and caused no end of difficulties to the British as it dominated their lines. In September 1914 there was a German artillery battery located a little to the north of here. Almost totally destroyed in these early clashes, the farm was eventually taken by the French 335th Regiment of Infantry on 18 April 1917. The obvious track to Folemprise Farm heads northeast between farm buildings and past a private house on the right to follow the GR12 route. The track you are on would have been the approximate position of the German front line looking south to the British lines clinging onto the edge of the high ground some 500 metres to the south where the line of trees are today.

From this vantage point there are good views of the high ground beyond the river, emphasising the advantage German gunners had in observing the British 60-pounder batteries that were in position south of the river. It is also from this point, where the ground falls away steeply to the river valley below, that an appreciation can be gained of why the British gunners had so much trouble in finding suitable locations from which to return fire. The German batteries were cleverly concealed and overlooked the whole of the valley below.

In just over a kilometre you will come to Folemprise Farm (2) which was in German hands and which also played host to a German artillery battery. The farm was taken by the French 25th Battalion of Infantry on 18 April 1917 after the German withdrawal, but totally destroyed over the course of the war. With the farm on your left take the track straight ahead of you towards the woods which leads gradually downhill to the old site of Rochefort Farm (3) at the junction of tracks. The farm was burnt down by the retiring Germans in 1917 and rebuilt further down the valley after the war. Turn right and head down the valley, keeping to the track that skirts the high ground on the right. The rebuilt Rochefort

Folemprise Farm.

Farm **(4)** is on your left. Eventually you will come to a junction with a minor road. **(5)** Stop here. Ahead of you the D885 snakes away towards the river and on the skyline is the flat expanse of the southern heights.

 To your right the open valley is bordered by woods and it was down

The view from the Verne family monument depicting the German advance of 20 September.

Southern heights of the Aisne valley

Gap in the British lines exploited

D885

Rochefort Farm

Line of the German advance on 20 September

The Verne family monument.

the valley you have just descended and through the woods on the right that the German *56* and *64 Infantry Regiments* broke through the British line on 20 September. Turn right up the minor road to reach the imposing memorial to Lieutenant Marcel Verne and Sergent Pilot Jean Pienaud, who were shot down and killed in their Farman F61 close to this spot on 24 March 1917.

They are both buried beneath the memorial which was erected by the Verne family. There is a bench here for the weary to enjoy the view. Once refreshed, continue steeply uphill keeping a look-out for the cave entrances on the right hand side, one of which is said to be quite extensive. Folemprise Farm soon comes into view and at the crossroads turn left and return to Rouge Maison Farm.

Once back at the farm you can take the track that runs southeast to visit the British line that clung to the edge of the high ground here. With the electricity sub-station on your left, follow the track as it skirts the wooded area on the right.

The track to the right of the electricity sub-station leads to La Fosse Marguet.

The British line was on your right **(6)** taking advantage of the woods and caves that are to be found on the slopes above Vailly. Continue until the track begins to cross the open ground of L'Abondin and heads towards the line of trees 300 metres ahead of you. **(7)** These are the woods that you would have seen on the right of the valley, when viewed from the Verne Family memorial, and where the Germans broke through the gap between the Wiltshires and Worcesters on 20 September. From here they began to enfilade the British lines and were less than a kilometre from 7 Brigade HQ, before they were pushed back. Retrace your steps and return to the farm.

ROUTE 3 – OLD CERNY VILLAGE

Suitable for:
Distance: 2 miles/6 km
Grade: Easy

In 1914 the village of Cerny-en-Laonnois consisted of about fifty buildings and some 200 inhabitants and was situated a little further to the north of the Chemin des Dames and the present day crossroads. Occupied by the Germans in September 1914, it was also home to a German field lazarette. The Sucrerie, which occupied the ground to the left of the road leading down to Vendresse, remained a German strongpoint until November 1917, when they withdrew after their defeat at Malmaison. The village was again in German hands after the

May offensive and not finally liberated until September 1918. The village was one of the numerous Aisne villages that were totally destroyed and reconstructed

The grass track leading down to the site of the old Cerny village.

Cerny village in 1918.

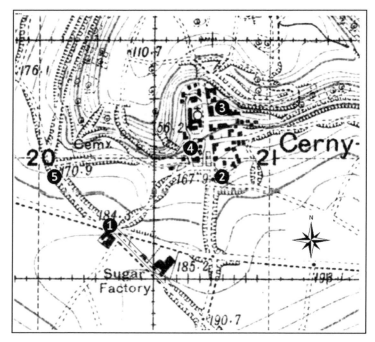

after the war. The new site is at the crossroads and has only sixty inhabitants, a population density of nine people per square kilometre.

From the crossroads **(1)** take the grassed track heading north east between two private houses. The track follows the line of the GR12 *Variante* and leads downhill to a T-junction of tracks. Ahead and below you is the Source St Remi, which still provides a regular flow of spring water today. Turn right at the junction and walk to the next junction. Stop here **(2)**. To your right is the old roadway that Lieutenant Colonel John Ponsonby of the 1/Coldstream Guards and his mixed force would have taken from the Sucrerie on the morning of 14 September. Ponsonby's map shows the path he and his party took into the village and his subsequent escape that night back to Vendresse. To the left is the old main street of Cerny village. It is along this main street that Ponsonby met the very concerned colonel commanding the German field

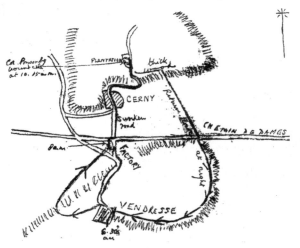

John Ponsonby's map of his escape from Cerny.

lazarette. Ponsonby assured him that he would be taking no offensive action against the German aid post and continued down the main street towards the plantation.

At the far end of the main street is the site of the former church and the

The war damaged village church and communal cemetery. The cemetery is all that remains today.

communal cemetery, the latter being still in use today and the only obvious vestige remaining of the former village. The village church would have been passed by Ponsonby's party on their way to the northern end of the village. Just before the cemetery a former village street leads off to the right **(3)**. Walk along here and see if you can spot any of the cellars of the houses that once stood here. Retrace your steps back to the cemetery and turn left back up the main street. You are looking for a narrow track on the right leading into the woods.

Along this track **(4)** there are countless shell holes and numerous cellars concealed in the undergrowth. Eventually the track passes close to a large cave entrance, which can be reached by a steep path leading down on the right. This may have been the Grotte de Cerny that is marked on old trench maps. Caution is required here and the author does not advise that the cave is entered.

Continue along the track to the junction, to the right is the source and straight ahead – up a slight rise – is the pathway you originally descended from the Cerny crossroads. Turn right here and continue straight ahead past the telecoms mast and the road barrier to the junction with the D967 **(5)**. Turn left past the farm to reach your vehicle at the Cerny crossroads.

The now over-grown track that was once a village street.

The cave entrance to the right of the track and the remnants of an old cellar wall

183

ROUTE 4 – THE CHEMIN DES DAMES AND PAISSY VILLAGE

Suitable for: 🚲 🍷

Distance: 5 miles/8 km
Grade: Moderate

Starting from the church at Moulins, this circular route visits the extreme right of the British line on the Chemin des Dames where the 1/West Yorkshires had their unfortunate introduction to the Aisne fighting. The route then heads south from the Poteau d'Ailles

crossroads to run along the eastern edge of the Paissy spur, to approach Paissy village from the north. After a visit to the churchyard and the village main street, we return to Moulins along the D888.

Park outside the church at Moulins **(1)** and take the Vendresse road – signposted D1840. On the morning of 14 September 1 Guards Brigade, having left Paissy at 5am, would have used this road on their way to Vendresse and Cerny. This is the Rue de la Fontaine, which soon brings you to a track on the right leading up to the communal cemetery **(2)**. For a description of the cemetery see **Car Tour 2**. After leaving the cemetery continue gradually uphill on the GR142, which skirts the eastern edge of Mont de Fléau. This is very probably the route taken by Lieutenant Jack Needham

The church at Moulins.

and the 1/Northamptons as they made their way up to the Chemin des Dames on the morning of 14 September. Across to your right the top of the Paissy church tower should be visible. The 2/KRRC were billeted at Paissy on the night of 13 September and their route to the Cerny crossroads the next morning would have taken them across the track you are now on, before they descended into the Troyon valley and up again to Cerny. As you climb the hill take the opportunity to glance behind you occasionally for the superb views that can be had of the country south of the Aisne.

A little over one kilometre from the cemetery, the GR142 joins the GR12, which appears on the left, and the track breaks out onto the open

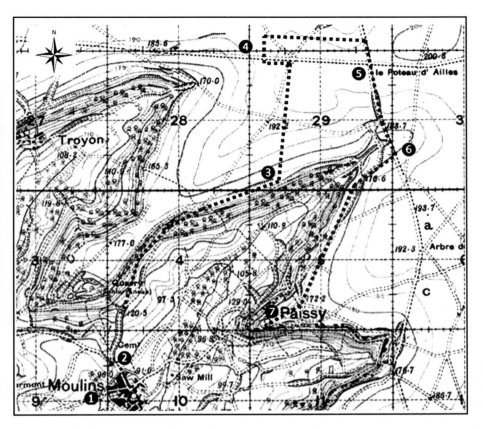

ground **(3)**. Stop here. Ahead is the line of the Chemin des Dames ridge, to the left is Cerny and to the right the Poteau d'Ailles crossroads, where the British line joined the left flank of the French Fifth Army. The Troyon valley is across to your left and you may just be able to see the line of trees marking its steep eastern edge.

Carry on along the track as it bends to the left and stop at the point where another track on the right comes in from the east. On 20 September, the Sherwood Foresters doubled across the ground in front of you, having first climbed the steep slope from Troyon, on their way to re-take the West Yorkshires' front line trenches which had been captured by the Germans.

Continue to the Chemin des Dames road and turn left. In 200 metres you will see a track on the other side of the road heading north. This is the track you are about to take but, before you do, walk on down to the memorial to **Sous-Lieutenant Louis Astoul (4)** who died near here fighting with the 70th Senegalese Infantry on 16 April 1917, yet another reminder of the disastrous Nivelle offensive. Retrace your steps

Troyon valley

Cerny

Chemin des
Dames

Poteau d'Ailles

British line running along the Chemin des
Dames and south of the Sucrerie at Cerny

Looking along the Chemin des Dames towards Cerny.

along the Chemin des Dames and in 130 metres turn left along the track towards the large barn. You are now back on the GR12 and on arrival at the barn, stop. Ahead of you is the Ailette valley and where the ground falls away was the former site of La Bovelle Farm. The farm was the limit of the 1/Queen's advance on 14 September. Ordered to advance towards Ailles, the line of trees you can see ahead of you is where the battalion first came under fire. Having taken the farm, the battalion soon found themselves surrounded and outnumbered. With the French falling back on their right, Lieutenant Colonel Dawson Warren ordered the battalion to retire to the line of the Chemin des Dames road and by 4.30pm they were back in touch with the French. Three days later the battalion lost their commanding officer and the battalion adjutant, Captain Charles Wilson. Both men are buried at Paissy Churchyard Cemetery. Command of the battalion fell to Captain Charles Watson DSO.

The Louis Astoul memorial on the Chemin des Dames.

Now take the track on the right leading towards Poteau d'Ailles Farm, which you can now see ahead of you. Whereas the British line along most this section of the Chemin des Dames was a little to the north of the road, just before the crossroads at Poteau d'Ailles **(5)** it began to fall away to the south as it met the left of the French Fifth Army. Turn right at the end of the track and after 250 metres cross straight over the Chemin des Dames. Stop at this point and

186

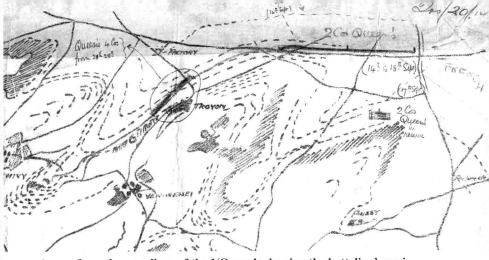

A map from the war diary of the 1/Queen's showing the battalion's position on the Chemin des Dames. Note the dotted line showing the limit of their advance on 14 September.

turn to look across to the right along the Chemin des Dames towards Cerny. This ground was the approximate position of the 1/West Yorkshires on the morning of 20 September. A and B Companies under the command of Major Alexander Ingles were in the front line positions, while Lieutenant Colonel Towsey and the remainder of the battalion were in support some distance behind. Now turn and look behind you; the line of trees behind the farm buildings is where the German attack was launched, breaking the resolve of the French colonial troops and the West Yorkshires.

Continue down the D102 towards Paissy – you should be able to see the top of the church steeple. Look straight ahead and Tour de Paissy Farm, which is visited in **Car Tour 2**, should come into view on the skyline. The ground to your right is the route over which the West Yorkshires retired and, from all accounts, continued down across the tree lined valley to Paissy village before they met the 4/Royal Irish Dragoon Guards. We are now going to follow the edge of that route as far as we can. As the road descends ignore the first track on the right and continue until the road begins to rise slightly. At this point a small track on the right **(6)** will take you along the edge of the wooded valley.

In just over a kilometre you will come to a junction of tracks. Before you take the right fork and head towards the church, look across to the left for a view of Tour de Paissy farm and look back along the track towards the Chemin des Dames. It is likely this track was also used by the 2/Royal Sussex and units of 2 Cavalry Brigade as they doubled up towards the Chemin des Dames to recover the trenches lost by the West Yorkshires. From the high point at Tour de Paissy farm, the whole

187

The memorial to Alfred Berger in Paissy Churchyard Cemetery.

incident was watched by Major General Edmund Allenby and his staff as it unfolded in front of them.

At the churchyard cemetery **(7)** you will find several French graves dating from 1915, some of which are in poor condition.

The CWGC headstones are to the left of the entrance in the north western corner. Details can be found in **Car Tour 2**. Leave the church and near the information panel you will find a steep flight of steps with a handrail. Descend the steps, but take care as, at the time of writing, several were in a poor state of repair. At the bottom turn left and then sharp right onto the main road. Alternatively you can walk down the road to the main street. Should you wish to visit the village and view the caves at the rear of the houses, this is your opportunity to do so.

The village is well served by information panels and there is also a short description in **Car Tour 2**. From Paissy it is just over a kilometre back to Moulins, using the D888.

Many of the caves in the village have been made habitable.

Appendix 1

THE AISNE CEMETERIES

There are approximately twenty-five cemeteries north and south of the river that contain casualties of the 1914 fighting. Below, in alphabetical order, are the locations and references to those cemeteries that are not featured in the text. The memorial at La Ferté-sous-Jouarre, although much further south, has been included as it commemorates so many of the Aisne dead of 1914. For more precise information on each cemetery visit the Commonwealth War Graves Commission website at: www.cwgc.org

Braine Communal Cemetery
Location: Braine is southeast of Chassemy on the D14. Once in the town turn left onto D1320 and follow signs for the cemetery.

Braine was taken by 1 Cavalry Brigade on 12 September and there are two casualties of that action here: **Captain G Springfield** and **Corporal Edward Medlam**. Thereafter, it was the home of No 5 Casualty Clearing Station and the majority of the seventy eight identified casualties are from that period, many of which are commemorated on special memorials. Buried here are **Captain Harry Ranken** VC who died of wounds on 25.9.14, **Lieutenant George Hutton** (19.9.14) from 1/Signal Company who drowned attempting to swim the river with a telephone cable and **Sergeant Herbert Shadbolt**, 2/Siege Battery, who died of wounds received after a premature explosion.

Chauny Communal Cemetery, British Extension
Location: From the town centre head north along Avenue Victor Hugo on the D937. Turn right onto Rue Ernest Renan and the communal cemetery is on the right hand side.

The cemetery was begun after the Armistice when casualties from the surrounding area were brought in; the majority are from 1918, but fifty-six of the identified 437 burials are from 1914. Five officers and eight men of the Sherwood Foresters are buried here, all casualties of the 20 September attack when the battalion re-took the West Yorkshires' trenches.

Ciry-Salsogne Communal Cemetery
The village is southeast of Sermoise and the cemetery is situated on the outskirts of the village

Three soldiers from 121 Battery, RFA are buried here. **Driver William Martin** and **Gunner William Wood**s were both probably killed by shellfire on 14 September, with **Gunner Francis Calow** dying of wounds two days later. At the time, 121/Battery were east of Sermoise near to the point where the Mezieres road bends southwest.

Crouy-Vauxrot French National Cemetery

Location: Crouy is northeast of Soissons on the D304. Enter Crouy on the Avenue du General Patton and turn left on Rue Mauruce Dupuis and in just over half a mile you will find the cemetery on the right.

There are now fifty burials here, twenty of which are unidentified. All were brought in after the Armistice, including twenty five Seaforth Highlanders who were previously buried at Bucy-le-Long and killed between 14 September and 4 October. Amongst the dead here is **Lieutenant Colonel Sir Evelyn Bradford**, the commanding officer of the Seaforths, who was more than twice the age of 18-year-old **Private Angus Paterson** who was killed on 15 September 1914.

La Ferté-sous-Jouarre Memorial

The memorial is situated in a small park on the south western edge of the town, on the south bank of the River Marne, just off the main road to Paris. The Memorial Register is kept at the Town Hall.

The La Ferté-sous-Jouarre Memorial commemorates nearly 4,000 officers and men of the British Expeditionary Force who died in August, September and the early part of October 1914 and who have no known grave. Names are listed on the memorial by regiments in order

of precedence, under the title of each regiment by rank, and under each
rank alphabetically

Longueval Communal Cemetery

Location: Longueval Barbonval is south of Bourg on the D976. Go
through the village and where the road takes a left hand bend bear right
along Rue des Forneaux.

The nineteen casualties here were all victims of shellfire who were
killed when the 9/Lancer's billets in the town were shelled on 29
September 1914. All are NCOs and enlisted men except **2/Lieutenant
George Taylor-Whitehead**.

Montcornet Military Cemetery

Location: From the town centre at Montcornet turn right, following the
signs for Rethel. Where the road forks, bear right and follow the
CWGC sign.

Over half the one hundred burials here are unidentified and the
cemetery holds casualties from 1914 and the 1918 German offensive.
There are only thirteen casualties here from the 1914 campaign and
includes men from the West Yorkshire Regiment, Rifle Brigade, KRRC,
Cameron Highlanders and the Black Watch.

Pargnan Churchyard

Location: Pargnan is just north of Oeuilly on the D893. The church and
its churchyard sits above the village.

There are six burials here, four of which are identified. This is very
much a gunners' plot, as all four identified casualties are from
26/Heavy Battery and 118/Battery. The youngest is **Gunner Bernard
Brandon** of 26/Heavy Battery, aged 17, killed on 25.9.14. **Gunner
John Ellison**, who was killed on 6.10.14, served with the same battery.
The two remaining casualties are from 118/Battery, **Driver William
Smith**, killed on 25.9.14 and **Driver James Chamberlin**, killed on
6.10.14.

Rozieres Churchyard

Location: The church is in the centre of the village of Rozieres-sur-
Crise, four kilometers south of Soissons.

There are twelve identified burials here all killed between 14-20 September. The youngest is 21-year-old **Private James Burns**, killed on 20.9.14 whilst serving with 2/Argyll & Sutherland Highlanders.

Serches Communal Cemetery
Location: Serches is on the D952 from Vénizel. The cemetery is on the left as you enter the village on the Rue de la Grenouillère.

There is only one casualty buried here, **Private Peter Thompson** 2/KOSB, who died on 22 September. Quite possibly he was buried here en route to the casualty collecting station at Le Mont de Soissons farm. The D952 was regularly swept by German shellfire.

Sissone British Cemetery
Location: The cemetery is east of Sissone on the D18.

The cemetery was made after the Armistice when casualties were brought in from the Chemin des Dames and surrounding area. There are ten 1914 casualties of the Aisne fighting here, a number of whom were killed in the fighting of 20 September.

Vauxbuin French National Cemetery
Location: The cemetery is four kilometers southwest of Soissons. It is best approached from the Soissons ring road – follow signs for Paris. The cemetery is on the busy N2.

This is a large French cemetery, situated adjacent to a German military cemetery. The British plot was made up after the Armistice from casualties brought in from surrounding areas. There are some 300 British burials here, over half of which are unidentified and only fifty-five are casualties from the Aisne in 1914. Here you will find 18-year-old **Second Lieutenant Gilbert Amos**, the KOSB subaltern who was killed at Missy on 14 September; and the two 1/Rifle Brigade casualties of 13 September mentioned by **Lieutenant Lionel Tennyson**: **Sergeant Charles Dorey**, the Platoon Sergeant of No 7 Platoon and **Rifleman Charles Spindler**.

Villers-en-Prayeres Communal Cemetery
Location: The village is south of Bourg on the D22. In the village turn right at the war memorial onto Rue des Marrionners.

There were two dressing stations in the village in 1914 and the thirty three men buried here will all probably have died of their wounds after evacuation from the battlefield.

Appendix II

ORDER OF BATTLE
BRITISH EXPEDITIONARY FORCE
September 1914

I CORPS – Lieutenant General Sir Douglas Haig

1ST DIVISION
General Officer Commanding – Major General S H Lomax

1 (Guards) Brigade
1/Coldstream
1/Scots Guards
1/Black Watch
1/Cameron Highlanders

2 Infantry Brigade
2/Royal Sussex Regiment
1/Loyal North Lancs
1/Northamptonshire Regt
2/Kings Royal Rifle Corps

3 Infantry Brigade
1/Queen's R West Surrey
1/South Wales Borderers
1/Gloucestershire Regt
2/Welch Regiment

Engineers
23/Field Company
26/Field Company
1/ Signal Company

Artillery
XXV Brigade
(113, 114, 115 Btrys)
XXVI Brigade
(116, 117, 118 Btrys)
XXXIX Brigade
(46, 51, 54 Btrys)
XLIII Howitzer Brigade
(30, 40, 57 Btrys)
26 Heavy Battery RGA

Field Ambulance
1/Field Ambulance
2/Field Ambulance
3/Field Ambulance

Divisional Mounted Troops
A Squadron 15/(The King's) Hussars
1/Cyclists' Company

2ND DIVISION
General Officer Commanding – Major General C C Monro

4 (Guards) Brigade
2/Grenadier Guards
2/Coldstream Guards
3/Coldstream Guards
1/Irish Guards

5 Infantry Brigade
2/Worcestershire Regt
2/Ox and Bucks L I
2/Highland L I
2/Connaught Rangers

6 Infantry Brigade
1/King's Liverpool Regt
2/South Staffordshire Regt
1/ Royal Berkshire Regt
1/King's Royal Rifle Corps

Engineers
5/Field Company
11/Field Company
2/ Signal Company

Artillery
XXXIV Brigade
(22, 50, 70 Btrys)
XXXVI Brigade
(15, 48, 71 Btrys)
XLI Brigade
(9, 16, 17 Btrys)
XLIV Howitzer Brigade
(47, 56, 60 Btrys)
35 Heavy Battery RGA

Field Ambulance
4/Field Ambulance
5/Field Ambulance
6/Field Ambulance

Divisional Mounted Troops
B Squadron 15/(The King's) Hussars
2/Cyclist Company

II CORPS – General Sir Horace Smith-Dorrien (after 17 August 1914)

3RD DIVISION
General Officer Commanding – Major General H I W Hamilton

7 Infantry Brigade
3/Worcestershire Regt
2/South Lancashire Regt
1/Wiltshire Regt
2/Royal Irish Rifles

8 Infantry Brigade
2/Royal Scots
2/Royal Irish Regt
4/Middlesex Regt
1/Gordon Highlanders

9 Infantry Brigade
1/Northumberland Fusiliers
4/Royal Fusiliers
1/Lincolnshire Regt
1/Royal Scots Fusiliers

Engineers
56/Field Company
57/Field Company
3/Signal Company

Artillery
XXIII Brigade
(107, 108, 109 Btrys)
XL Brigade
(6, 23, 49 Btrys)
XLII Brigade
(29, 41, 45 Btrys)
XXX Howitzer Brigade
(128, 129, 130 Btrys)
48 Heavy Battery RGA

Field Ambulance
7/Field Ambulance
8/Field Ambulance
9/Field Ambulance

Divisional Mounted Troops
C Squadron 15/(The Kings) Hussars
3/Cyclist Company

5H DIVISION
General Officer Commanding – Major General Sir C Fergusson

13 Infantry Brigade
2/King's Own Scottish B
2/Duke of Wellington's
1/Queen's R West Kent
2/King's Own Yorkshire LI

14 Infantry Brigade
2/Suffolk Regt
1/East Surrey Regt
1/Duke of Cornwalls LI
2/Manchester Regt

15 Infantry Brigade
1/Norfolk Regt
1/Bedfordshire Regt
1/ Cheshire Regt
1/Dorsetshire Regt

Engineers
59/Field Company
17/Field Company
5/Signal Company

Artillery
XV Brigade
(11, 52, 80 Btrys)
XXVII Brigade
(119, 120, 121 Btrys)
XXVIII Brigade
(122, 123, 124 Btrys)
VIII Howitzer Brigade
(37, 61, 65 Btrys)
108 Heavy Battery RGA

Field Ambulance
13/Field Ambulance
14/Field Ambulance
15/Field Ambulance

Divisional Mounted Troops
A Squadron 19/(Queen Alexandra's Own) Royal Hussars
5/Cyclist Company

III CORPS – Major General W P Pulteney (formed in France 31 August 1914)

4TH DIVISION
General Officer Commanding – Major General T D'O Snow
(Landed in France on 22/23 August 1914)

10 Infantry Brigade
1/Royal Warwickshire Regt
2/Seaforth Highlanders
1/Royal Irish Fusiliers
2/Royal Dublin Fusiliers

11 Infantry Brigade
1/Somerset L I
1/East Lancashire Regt
1/Hampshire Regt
1/Rifle Brigade

12 Infantry Brigade
1/King's Own
2/Lancashire Fusiliers
2/Inniskilling Fusiliers
2/Essex Regt

Artillery
XIV Brigade
(39, 68, 88 Btrys)
XXIX Brigade
(125, 126, 127 Btrys)
XXXII Brigade
(27, 134, 135 Btrys)
XXXVII Howitzer Brigade
(31, 35, 55 Btrys)
31 Heavy Battery RGA

Engineers
7/Field Company
9 Field Company
4/Signal Company

Field Ambulance
10/Field Ambulance
11/Field Ambulance
12/Field Ambulance

Divisional Mounted Troops
B Squadron 19/(Queen Alexandra's Own) Royal Hussars
4/Cyclist Company

6TH DIVISION
General Officer Commanding – Major General J L Keir
(Landed in France on 9 September)

16 Infantry Brigade
1/ East Kent Regt
1/Leicestershire Regt
1/King's Shropshire L I
2/York and Lancaster Regt

17 Infantry Brigade
1/Royal Fusiliers
1/North Staffordshire Regt
2/Leinster Regt
3/Rifle Brigade

18 Infantry Brigade
1/West Yorkshire Regt
1/East Yorkshire Regt
2/Notts & Derby Regt
2/Durham L I

Artillery
II Brigade
21,42,53 Brtys
XXIV Brigade
110,11,112 Btrys
XXXVIII Brigade
24,34,72 Brtys
XII Howitzer Brigade
43,86,87 Brtys

Engineers
12/Field Company
38 Field Company
6/Signal company

Field Ambulance
16/Field Ambulance
17/Field Ambulance
18/Field Ambulance

Divisional Mounted Troops
C Squadron 19/(Queen Alexandra's Own) Royal Hussars
6/Cyclist Company

CAVALRY CORPS – Major General E H Allenby

1 Cavalry Brigade
2/Dragoon Guards (Queens Bays)
5/ Princess Charlotte's) Dragoon Guards
(11/(Prince Albert's Own)Hussars

2 Cavalry Brigade
4/(Royal Irish) Dragoon Guards
9/(Queen's Royal) Lancers
18/(Queen Mary's Own) Hussars

3 Cavalry Brigade
4/ (Queen's Own) Hussars
5/(Royal Irish) Lancers
16/(The Queen's) Lancers

4 Cavalry Brigade
Composite Household Cavalry Regiment
6/Dragoon Guards (Carabiniers)
3/(King's Own) Hussars

ENGINEERS
1/Field Squadron RE
1/Signal Troop

HORSE ARTILLERY
III Brigade RHA
D and E Batteries
III Brigade Ammunition Column
VII Brigade RHA
I and L Batteries
VII Brigade Ammunition Column

FIELD AMBULANCE
1/Cavalry FA
2/Cavalry FA
3/Cavalry FA
4/Cavalry FA

5 Cavalry Brigade
2/Dragoons (Royal Scots Greys)
12/(Prince of Wales's Own) Lancers
20/Hussars

ENGINEERS
4/Field Troop
5/Signal Troop

HORSE ARTILLERY
J Battery RHA and Ammunition Column

FIELD AMBULANCE
5/Cavalry FA

19th Infantry Brigade
(formed from lines of communication troops at Valenciennes on 22 August)

General officers commanding
Initially the brigade was under the independent command of Major General L G Drummond. Colonel B E Ward assumed command of the brigade after Drummond was wounded on 27 August, relinquishing command on 3 September 1914, when Brigadier General F Gordon was appointed.

Battalions
1/Devonshire Regiment
2/Royal Welch Fusiliers
1/Cameronians
1/Middlesex Regiment
2/Argyll and Sutherland Highlanders

Infantry brigades were generally deployed as part of an infantry division. However the role of 19 Brigade in August 1914 was to hold key towns and bridges along the route that connected the BEF to its supply bases on the coast, hence the term lines of communication. At Mons, for example, the 1/Middlesex were ordered to hold bridges and locks over the canal in anticipation of the general advance. In this manner it became embroiled in the retreat. On 25 August they were called upon to support the cavalry near Haussy before moving on to Solesmes and Le Cateau. At Le Cateau, the brigade was used on the right flank and was in action with the 2/Suffolks on the Montay Spur.

However, although it remained independent as such, it served as reinforcement troops for the remainder of the retreat and was later attached to the 6th Division

The brigade continued in this role until May 1915, when it finally found a permanent home with the 27th Infantry Division.

Appendix III

ORDER OF BATTLE
GERMAN IMPERIAL ARMY
September 1914

The following is a basic order of battle for the four German armies that were involved in the fighting that took place in the BEF sector on the Aisne between 15 September and early October 1914.

FIRST ARMY
General Alexander von Kluck

II Corps   von Linsingen
                 3rd and 4th Divisions
III Corps   von Lochow
                 5th and 6th Divisions
IV Corps   Sixt von Armin
                 7th and 8th Divisions
IX Corps   von Quast
                 17th and 18th Divisions
III Reserve Corps   von Beseler
                 5th Reserve and 6th Reserve Divisions
IV Reserve Corps   von Gronau
                 7th Reserve and 22nd Reserve Divisions

10th Landwehr Brigade

11th Landwehr Brigade

27th Landwehr Brigade

SECOND ARMY
General Karl von Bülow

Guard Corps   von Plettenberg
                 1st Guard and 2nd Guard Divisions
VII Corps   von Elaer
                 13th and 14th Divisions
X Corps   von Emmich
                 19th and 20th Divisions
Guard Reserve Corps   von Gallwitz
                 1st Guard and 3rd Guard Reserve Divisions
X Reserve Corps   von Eben
                 2nd Guard Reserve and 19th Reserve Divisions
XVII Corps

SEVENTH ARMY
General von Heeringen

XIV Corps	von Heiningen
	28th and 29th Divisions
XV Corps	von Deimling
	30th and 39th Divisions
VII Reserve Corps	von Zwehl
	13th Reserve and 14th Reserve Divisions
IX Reserve Corps	von Benzino
	17th Reserve and 18th Reserve Divisions

CAVALRY CORPS

1st Cavalry Corps	von Richthofen
	5th Cavalry Division
	Guard Cavalry Division
	11th Jaeger Battalion
	12th Jaeger Battalion
	13th Jaeger Battalion
2nd Cavalry Corps	von der Marwitz
	2nd Cavalry Division
	4th Cavalry division
	9th Cavalry Division
	3rd Jaeger Battalion
	4th Jaeger Battalion
	7th Jaeger Battalion
	9th Jaeger Battalion
	10th Jaeger Battalion

Bibliography

Primary Sources:
The National Archives:

1/East Surrey War Diary. TNA WO 95/1563.

4th Division War Diary, TNA WO 95/1439.

2/Battalion Lancashire Fusiliers War Diary, TNA WO 95/1495.

8/Field Ambulance War Diary, TNA WO 95/1407.

2/Connaught Rangers War Diary, TNA WO 95/1347.

I Corps War Diary, TNA WO 95/588.

11/Hussars War Diary, TNA WO 95/1109.

1/Loyal North Lancs War Diary, TNA WO 95/1270.

1/Queen's Own Cameron Highlanders War Diary. TNA WO95/1246.

1/West Yorkshire War Diary, TNA WO 95/1618.

POW Report, TNA WO 161/95/98.

Imperial War Museum Department of Documents:

Private Papers of Lord Tennyson. IWM Dept of Documents 76/21/1.

Private Papers of C L Brereton. IWM dept of Documents 86/30/1.

Private Papers of G A Kempthorne. IWM Dept. of Documents 79/17/1.

The Private Papers of J G Stennett. IWM Dept of Documents 6655.

Private Papers of C Rainbird. IWM Dept of Documents 02/39/1.

Other sources:

Paterson, *War Diary of 24th (SWB)*. SWB Museum Archive.W.18.66.

The Diary of Major G Ward. SWB Museum Archive W.2.48.

Private Diary of Major Bernard Gordon Lennox, Grenadier Guards Archive.

The Diary of JBW Pennyman. Teeside Archives U.PEN/7/150.

The Personal Diary of Kenneth Godsell, RE Archive.

Typescript Diary of Gerald Whittuck, Somerset Light Infantry Archive.

Published and Secondary Sources:

Anglesey, The Marquess of: *A History of the British Cavalry 1816–1919* (Vol. 7), Leo Cooper, 1973–1982.

Astil, Edwin (ed): *The Great War Diaries of Brigadier General Alexander Johnston 1914-1917*, Pen & Sword 2007.

Bloem, Walter: *The Advance From Mons*, Tandem, 1967.

Bridges, Tom: *Alarms and Excursions*, Longmans, 1938.

Coleman, Frederick: *From Mons to Ypres with General French*, A L Burt Company, 1916.

Craster, JM: *Fifteen Rounds a Minute*, Pen & Sword 2012.

Dolbey, RV: *A Regimental Surgeon in War and Prison*, John Murray, 1917.

Edmonds, JE: *Military Operations France and Belgium 1914 Vol. 1*, Macmillan, 1926.

Laing, H Evans and N: *The 4th (Queen's Own) Hussars in the Great War*, Gale and Polden, 1920.

Farndale, General Sir M: *History of the Royal Regiment of Artillery - Western Front*, Royal Artillery Institution 1986.

Gardner, Nikolas: *Trial by Fire*, Praeger, 2003.

Gibb, H: *Record of the 4th Royal Irish Dragoon Guards in the Great War 1914–1918*, Canterbury, 1925.

Gillard, Brian: *Good Old Somersets – An Old Contemptible Battalion in 1914*, Matador 2004.

Gillion, Stair: *The KOSB in the Great War*, Thomas Nelson, 1930.

Gliddon, Gerald: *VCs Handbook*, Sutton, 2005.

Gleichen, Count Edward: *The Doings of the Fifteenth Infantry Brigade,* Blackwood, 1917.

Haldane, Sir Aylmer: *A Brigade of the Old Army 1914*. Edward Arnold, 1920.

Hamilton, Lord E: *The First Seven Divisions*, Hurst & Blackett, 1916.

Hanbury-Sparrow, AA: *The Land Locked Lake*, Arthur Barker 1932.

Kipling, Rudyard: *The Irish Guards in the Great War- Volume 1: The 1st Battalion*, Leonaur 2007.

Lowry, Gerald: *From Mons to 1933*, Simpkin and Marshall 1933.

Lucy, JF: *There's a Devil in the Drum*, Faber and Faber 1938.

MacDonald, Lynn: *1914*, Michael Joseph 1987.

Marden, Major General T: *A Short History of the 6th Division*, Hugh Rees 1920.

Maloney, CV: *Invicta, With the 1st Battalion The Queen's Own Royal West Kent Regiment in The Great War*, Nisbet & Co., 1923.

Needham, Evelyn J: *The First Three Months*, Gale and Polden 1936.

Osburn, Arthur: *Unwilling Passenger*, Faber and Faber 1932.

Ponsonby, F, *The Grenadier Guards In The Great War of 1914–1918*, Macmillan 1920.

Pritchard, Major General H L (ed): *History of The Corps Of Royal Engineers (Volume 5)*, Institute of Royal Engineers, 1951.

Ross of Bladensburg, Sir J: *The Coldstream Guards 1914–1918*, Oxford University Press, 1928.

Sheffield G and Bourne, J (eds): *Douglas Haig War Diaries and Letters 1914–1918*, Orion, 2005.

Simpson, CR: *,History of the Lincolnshire Regiment 1914-1918*, The Medici Society 1931.

Taylor, J: *The 2nd Royal Irish Rifles in the Great War*, Four Courts 2005.

War Office, *Battle of the Aisne 13th -15th September, 1914 – Tour of the Battlefield*, H M Stationary Office 1934.

Wyrall, Everard : *The Gloucestershire Regiment in the War 1914–1918*, Methuen, 1931.

Wyrall, Everard: *The History of the Duke of Cornwall's Light Infantry 1914–1919*, Methuen & Co 1932.

Wyrall, Everard :*The Diehards in the Great War*, Harrisons and Sons, 1926.

Wylly, HC: *History of the 1st & 2nd Battalions The Leicestershire Regiment in the Great War*, Gale and Polden 1928.

Articles:

Captain H A Baker, History of the 7th Field Company, RE, During the War 1914–1918, *RE Journal*, June 1932.

Brigadier General C J Griffin, Crossing the Aisne, *The Lancashire Fusiliers Annual 1916*, Number XXVIII.

W A Synge, From the Marne to The Aisne - The Diary of an Infantry Subaltern, *Army Quarterly*, January and May 1935.

Brigadier General G Walker, From the Curragh to the Aisne, 1914, *R E Journal*, April 1919.

Major B K Young, The Diary of an RE Subaltern with the BEF in 1914, *RE Journal*, December 1933.

INDEX

2 Connaught Rangers, 63,73,75-7, 81-2,117,119,120,145,154,158.
2 Duke of Wellingtons, 52.
2 Essex, 34.
2 Grenadier Guards, 75,77,87.
2 Highland Light Infantry, 86,119, 120.
2 KOSB, 43-4,48-50,142,145.
2 KOYLI, 52.
2 KRRC, 94-5,104,167,170,184.
2 Lancashire Fusiliers, 33,34,45,130-1, 138.
2 Manchester, 35,45.
2 Notts and Derby, 124,126,164,185.
2 Ox and Bucks Light Infantry, 81, 87,154.
2 Royal Fusiliers, 59,60.
2 Royal Irish, 56,58,60,115,144.
2 Royal Irish Rifles, 67,68-70.
2 Royal Scots, 56,58,60,144.
2 South Lancashire, 116-7.
2 South Staffordshire, 117.
2 Royal Sussex, 94,95-6,97,163,170.
2 Worcestershire, 85.
3 Coldstream Guards, 77,80,82.
3 Worcestershire, 113.
4 Middlesex, 58,60.

Cavalry Units:
2 Dragoons (Scots Greys), 63.
4 Hussars, 55,142.
4 Royal Irish Dragoon Guards, 80,81, 91-2,125,158,159,160,169,187.
9 Lancers, 125,162,164.
11 Hussars, 81.
12 Lancers, 63,66.
15 Hussars, 26,80.
20 Hussars, 11,63,66.

Field Ambulance:
1 FA, 107,161.
2 FA, 107.
3 Cavalry FA, 89,153.
3 FA, 106-7.
4 FA, 89,90,153.

5 FA, 88.
6 FA, 88.
7 FA, 71.
8 FA, 70,71,147.
10 FA, 30,38,141,172.
11 FA, 38,40,141.
15 FA, 53.

Royal Artillery Brigades:
XIV, 32,34.
XV, 45.
XXIII, 117.
XXV, 102-3.
XXX, 115.
XXXIV, 84.
XXXVI, 78.
XL, 58.
XLI, 81.
XLII, 67.

Batteries:
1 Siege, 153.
2 Siege, 160.
16B, 81,88,161.
31B, 34.
35B, 81.
37B, 45.
44B, 81.
48B, 58,67.
49B, 58.
61B, 45.
68B, 32,35,36,175.
71B, 78,81.
113B, 107,108.
114B, 102,103.
115B, 162.
116B, 103.
130B, 67.
135B, 170.

Royal Engineers:
2 Bridging Train, 51,141.
5 Field Company, 73,158.
9 Field Company, 13,29,36,52.
11 Field Company, 73,158.
17 Field Company, 7,39,41,43,45,141.